...and this is the bathroom!

...and this is
the bathroom!

HOW TO REALLY
SELL REAL ESTATE

Andy Kane

PALADIN PRESS
BOULDER, COLORADO

Other books by Andy Kane:

Care and Feeding of Tenants
Mastering the Art of Male Supremacy
Tenant's Revenge

. . . and this is the bathroom!
How To Really Sell Real Estate
by Andy Kane
Copyright © 1989 by Andy Kane

ISBN 0-87364-524-3
Printed in the United States of America

Published by Paladin Press, a division of
Paladin Enterprises, Inc., P.O. Box 1307,
Boulder, Colorado 80306, USA.
(303) 443-7250

Direct inquiries and/or orders to the above address.

Illustrations by Steve Soeffing

Contents

Preface

You have probably seen a movie or two with an unusual title. If you watch closely for an hour and a half and listen to every word uttered by every actor, you will eventually hear the title casually mentioned. I'm going to save you the anguish and explain the title of this book.

In my geographical area, I am fairly well known. I have been featured in a cover story in the magazine section of the Sunday paper, with a readership of several million. I have been the subject of many front-page articles in both daily papers. I have appeared regularly on television and radio, and all this exposure has been real estate oriented. I have extensive education and training in real estate. I have designations from various national real estate and appraisal organizations. With this background, I assume that when a homeowner calls me to list his abode, he does so because of my extensive real estate background, superior sales ability, and name recognition in the area.

When I arrive at the appointed hour at the homeowner's residence, he and his lovely wife meet me at the front door. He says, "This is the vestibule..." turns and walks (shuffle, shuffle) into the living room, followed by his lovely wife (click,

click of high heels), followed by me (clump, clump). He then
says, "And this is the living room . . ." (shuffle, shuffle, click,
click, clump, clump) "And this is the kitchen . . ." (shuffle,
shuffle, click, click, clump, clump) "And this is the bathroom!"

Now, I might have been confused when I entered the living
room or dining room. The kitchen was pretty obvious. But
when you enter the only 5'×8' room with a sink, tub, and
crapper, *what else could it be*! Yet this homeowner, who has
selected me because of my superior sales skill, knowledge,
and community recognition, feels compelled to explain the
function of each room. If he did not have confidence in my
ability to distinguish various rooms, why did he call me?

I have even tried to make the whole procedure look
ridiculous to the homeowner by asking questions. As we
entered the attic and he said, "And this is the attic," I said,
"Wait a minute, I thought we were in the cellar." He said,
without hesitation, "No, this is the attic." I mumbled, "I saw
the stairs and I thought since there were stairs, we were in
the basement. I guess if there is no furnace, hot water heater
or abandoned refrigerators, it must be the attic. Sorry." (He
listed the house with me.)

The real reason people tell you what room you are in, when it would be obvious to most living human beings, is because they cannot think of anything else to say. Think back; if you have been in the real estate business for longer than four hours, you have probably had a homeowner go through the same spiel, or even worse, you have probably used the same phrases to show a prospective buyer a dream house.

I made up my mind to never again say, "And this is the...." Never, ever, ever again, because it is so stupid! The next house I showed, I did not say a thing as we entered the living room. I acted like a mime. I just nodded my head up and down and smiled and did not say one word! The *buyer* looked around and said, "And this is the living room!" I give up. I guess there are just some mysteries in life that we will never fully understand!

Acknowledgments

Several people were instrumental in my entering the real estate field, the first of whom was my mother. She taught me the rental business at about the same time she taught me to tie my shoes, and that sort of got me hooked on property. Walt Streeter, a broker who specialized in apartment houses, and Sid Shapiro, an attorney who closed some of my early deals, let me float their commissions and fees to get started. Jimmy Brenna was the broker I started selling with. I'm still surprised I didn't give him a heart attack or an ulcer! Bob Ellwell and Bob Wilson of our local Real Estate Board, and Ross Amic of the Department of State, were a storehouse of information regarding the real estate industry rules and regulations. Without their help and information, I would have had to spend a fortune on research. Evie and Lucille, my valuable secretaries, and Doreen, our part-time *sex*retary, were worth their weight in gold. Without these people, and many others, this book would not have been possible. Thanks!

Introduction

Another book on selling real estate! There must be thousands, and I think I have bought every one. I have also attended every sales seminar given by evangelistic podium thumpers selling their books, tapes, and videos. I won't say that I did not gain a little knowledge from these books, seminars, and videos, but, all in all, they were pretty much the same. This book is *not* like any of them.

Some of the techniques in this book may not be for you; some may be considered by many to be dishonest, underhanded, fraudulent, or distasteful. I do not consider this to be true. I feel if you do not use every trick in the world to sell your listing, you are not doing the job the client hired you for and you should get out of the business. When the client hires you to sell his shack, he wants it sold! Now! He does not care what you do to sell it, he just wants it sold, fast, and for the biggest buck it will bring. It's just like the "Godfather" hiring a hit man to take care of a problem client. He wants it done efficiently, and he is only interested in the end result.

I do not suggest any illegal action to sell Mr. Joe Home-owner's abode, because a real estate license is hard to come by. You should never do anything that would jeopardize your livelihood or that of your broker.

In this book, I give you a foolproof, easy way to double your listing volume with the stroke of a pen. Now that's worth the price of the book alone! In addition to that, you will find many other techniques that will enable you to rise above your fellow salesmen (unless they buy this book, too) and enjoy the finer things in life.

Many times other salespeople have indicated that some of my techniques (using shills, threats of foreclosure, etc.) are unprofessional. I disagree. Professional means doing something and getting paid for it. Since what I do (and recommend in this book) is *never* illegal and I get paid for it, it must be professional. Since I do it more than most "professionals," I get paid more. My logic is that I am more professional than the "professionals" who consider my techniques unprofessional.

I feel the techniques and schemes in this book will greatly benefit you. As evidence of that, let me elaborate on my past. I entered the real estate profession in late 1969 as a part-time salesperson working two days a week (Tuesday and Thursday). Two years later, I owned three real estate companies that employed twenty-one salespeople and three office people.

Since I have operated my own business, seven of my salespeople, who came to me untrained from professions unrelated to real estate (construction worker, union boss, fireman, mailman, mental hospital outpatient), have gained enough experience to start their own real estate companies! My technique must work, or these guys would be back to hauling bricks, breaking noses, putting out fires, losing mail, or cutting out paper dolls!

Selling real estate is one of America's most prestigious occupations. All you really need to get started is a few listing pads, some purchase offers, and a sharp pencil. The opportunity to get rich is unlimited. Compare selling real estate to a corner Mom and Pop grocery store. To get started, you need storefront, coolers, beer license, health permit, inventory, shelves, and hired help. It will probably cost $50,000 before you could open for business. You can get into the real estate business for pocket change. In the grocery business, bread gets stale, milk sours, lettuce rots, and people steal. Houses don't go stale, sour, rot, or get stolen. The grocer has to maintain an inventory at his own expense. Your inventory of listings, usually worth several million bucks, is supplied, free of charge, by your clients. How much easier could it be?

You don't need a special education to be competitive in real estate. I have blundered along fairly successfully with just a high school diploma. A college degree probably wouldn't hurt, but it probably won't put a much larger sum of money in your pocket each year. Your best bet is to devote any extra time you have to educational requirements for maintaining or improving your license (salesman to broker, etc.) and other courses directly related to the real estate profession.

Since I have been in the real estate business for zillions of years, many unusual, humorous, and traumatic events have occurred. Many of these have been included at the end of appropriate chapters for your enjoyment. No peeking! Just like your mother always said, you're to eat your meat and potatoes before dessert!

Now, turn the page and start making big money!

What It Takes

Selling real estate may look easy, but believe me, it's not. There are long hard hours to get started, unreasonable and downright rotten clients, and brokers who are demanding slave drivers. There are do-gooder groups who will throw obstacles in your path, license training, and tests to pass. Possibly as high as 50 percent of the people entering the field fail, and even more hang on with just a sale or two a year to keep the wolf away from their doors. I estimate that 10 percent of the people in the field make a good, comfortable living.

If you know people in the business, or you are in the business now, you can probably visualize the salesmen who are in that 10 percent. Think about it; what qualities do they have? I guarantee they have the following:

1. *PMA is number one!* A Positive Mental Attitude is a must in real estate, as it is to be successful in any business. If you don't have PMA and you cannot develop it, you are through before you start. Get a job driving a bus or waiting tables because you *cannot*, under any circumstances, succeed without PMA.

2. *Knowledge of their product.* Whether it is selling cars,

computers, siding, or houses, you must know your product. To get started in real estate, you should know a little about a house.

Unless you lived in a jungle hut all your life, you know what a furnace looks like, as well as a dishwasher, a disposal, and a garage door opener. You can get started knowing only the basics, but you should devote a certain amount of your free time to reading home repair books, visiting construction sites, talking to tradesmen, visiting home improvement shows, and in general, building your knowledge of homes and buildings. Some part-time work in the building trades will increase your knowledge while putting some groceries on your table.

3. *A desire to make big bucks!* This is a high priority and would be number one, except you need the previous items to succeed at making money. The real estate business is fantastic for making money. You are not restrained to what you can make, like a factory worker is. A good salesman does not have any idea what the year's annual take will be. He really does not want to know. He is shooting for the moon. Although he may only make a few hundred thousand dollars this year, he does not want any limit in advance. That's the joy of being a salesman.

A factory worker can sit down with a pen and, giving himself maximum raises every six months and a cost of living increase to match inflation, calculate the amount of money he will make the rest of his working life! Of course, he may die of poisoning from some industrial waste he inhales, or the plant may be phased out and he will end up in the scrap heap of used employees. A good salesman will not want any restraints placed on his income.

4. *Personality and visibility.* A good salesman is well known and can deal with people. He stands out in a crowd and he relates to all walks of life. He can carry on a conversation with Louie Lugnuts at the corner garage or Dr. Big Bucks at the country club. If you ask ten people in the area if they know him, five will say they do. He makes friends anywhere he goes. You must have a good personality to be a top pro-

ducer. If you don't have one, or can't pretend to have one, get the yellow pages and look for a Dale Carnegie course.

5. *Self-starter.* If you are the type that has to have a boss tell you to get off your tail, you won't make it in this business. A top dog gets moving at dawn and keeps it up all day, everyday. He does not need anyone to tell him to get to work. He lives and breathes real estate. Real estate to him is like a fresh glass of blood to Dracula. A good self-starter plans his time and is off like a racehorse every day. Self-starting is a requirement, not an option in selling.

Did I leave anything out? We have PMA, knowledge, bucks and smiles, self-starter. But you say, "What about helping people?"

Helping people is not important. You want to devote your time to helping *you*, Number One. If by some chance you help others while you are helping Number One, that's permissible. Just don't go out and help people for the fun of it. If you like helping for free, you can always get involved with a religious group or the Salvation Army. They are always looking for volunteers. You should devote all your energy to feathering the nest of Number One!

If you feel that you have the qualifications of a real estate salesperson, get moving today. I have only one regret when it comes to my career and that is I waited until I was in my thirties to get a real estate license.

THE REAL ESTATE CAREER CAPER

How did I get into real estate sales? I saw a four-family apartment house for sale in the newspaper. I stopped over to see the realtor who had it listed and saw the workings of his "office." He was a small operator, working out of his basement with two or three salespeople. He was driving a shiny new Cadillac, wore a custom-made suit, and smoked foot-long imported cigars. I started thinking. If he can do it, why can't I? I got a license with him and lived happily ever after! It was like going to the store for one thing and bringing home something else. I went out to buy an apartment house and came home with a new career.

Picking An Office

"Nothing to it," you say. There was this big ad on TV. . .
Fantastic Realty, an independently owned office of the Super
Fantastic World Wide chain of real estate companies, is
offering a career opportunity to a few select individuals who
possess the unusual qualities they are looking for. Actually,
most companies will take anyone who has two arms and legs,
or at least some of the aforementioned plus a prosthesis
(wooden leg, hook in place of a hand, etc). They will give
them a try, and if they don't pan out, they kick them out the
door and try another warm body. You, being a cut above the
rest (you bought my book!), can pick and choose the company
that is right for you.

Some of the important features you should consider when
selecting a broker to work with are:

1. *Location*. That magic word. If you live ten miles from
your office, you will spend a lot of time jockeying your jalopy
when you could spend that time in a more productive manner, such as prospecting, reviewing listings, or talking to
clients. Only truckers and taxicab drivers get paid by the mile.
Pick an office that suits your needs and is conveniently close
to home.

2. *Type of office.* Many offices specialize in certain fields: residential, commercial, investment, suburbs, city, slums, plazas, recreational, etc. If there is a field you would like to pursue and a company specializes in that area, you may want to join that firm.

3. *Climate.* If you live in Oswego, New York, where the temperature is "warm" at five degrees below zero, eight months out of the year, and a "little" snow usually means being quarantined in your hut for three or four days, you might consider a more tropical climate. It's hard to sell real estate from your home while shut in with snowdrifts higher than your roof. This is unproductive time. If you relocate to a more suitable climate, you gain several months of selling time.

I have an acquaintance who became fed up with mittens, galoshes, snow tires, and blue fingers. He became an agent in Tampa, Florida, and specialized in selling time-share condos, vacation villas, and retirement homes in a "clothing optional" resort community. His day consisted of dragging his lawn chair over to the pool, rubbing on some tanning lotion (or recruiting a "lovely" to rub it on!), setting up his brochures and display, ordering a mint julep from the poolside bar, and plugging in his portable phone. On slow days he put his radio-controlled model boat in the pool. On the mast was a small sign that read, "Time-share condo, $1,500!" He would direct the boat to potential clients and when he got their attention, he would beckon them over to the edge of the pool and give his pitch.

If there is an area where you feel at home—resort, golf community, historic, etc.—you will probably do better in that environment than you would somewhere else.

4. *Commission splits.* There are various splits ranging from 50/50 to 100 percent. I have even offered one salesperson a 105 percent split! I would have actually lost 5 percent, if she came to work with us. Why would I do this? There were some other figures involved in the decision, like 38–24–36! She was a reigning national beauty queen! I figured she would not sell a hell of a lot, but she would draw clients to the office, and the other salespeople working on a 50/50 split would sell the homes. I would lose on her but make it on the others.

If advertising and office expenses are paid by the broker, a 50/50 split is reasonable. In the case of the 100 percent split, you pay all your own expenses. Many times the 100 percent split works out to give you less of an annual net income than the 50/50 split. Look for something you feel comfortable with and go for it!

5. *Compatibility.* You will probably spend more time with the office gang than you spend with your lovely spouse. Be careful. If you feel friction, resentment, or unfriendliness, you may have a hard row to hoe!

Many salespeople are vultures. They are not doing well, their back is against the wall, their child support is late, that Cadillac has three payments due, and they need dog food for the puppy or it will eat them. This misfit may try to grab your clients and list or sell to them. An office where this occurs is not a productive place to hang your hat and should be avoided.

6. *Clone Realty.* If you have served in the military and like wearing a uniform, you may like working at Clone Realty. At Clone Realty, all the salespeople look the same. Even the girls wear blazers—all the same style, same color underwear, same color socks. Oh, you can tell them apart. They all have tags on their lapels with their names on them! They also pay a small portion of every sale to the mother company, and this gets them TV spots nationally, which may attract a transferee homebuyer moving from East Podunk to Your Town. It also

pays for a host of mucky mucks to smoke big cigars at the national headquarters of Clone Realty. If you like this atmosphere compared to a locally owned company, there is not much harm in "joining up."

7. *Small vs. big companies.* Not franchise types, just big in a local sense. Small, seven to twenty people, maybe one or two offices, versus big, four hundred or more, ten to twelve locations spread around town. I personally prefer small. Your chance of grabbing a walk-in client in an office of ten people is ten to one; in an office of fifty, it's fifty to one.

I am a firm believer that success is up to you. It's how hard *you* work and follow through. I do not believe it is in proportion to the size of the company you work for. You can be a top producer in any company just by getting off your tail.

You may wish to add a few more conditions to this list to fit your specifications. Keep in mind that most people work best in comfortable, friendly surroundings. Pick your starting broker carefully, and keep in mind that you do not have to stay there forever. If you find things look better somewhere else, you can always transfer, but it's better to start off right, if possible. If you start at ABC Realty and move to XYZ Realty in two years, a lot of your referrals will still go to ABC. They will probably say you died, but John Jones of ABC is still alive and taking care of your referrals.

Your Name

Now that's getting really personal isn't it? Your name is your name! Maybe it's Zigfried Hennersdorfer, Dimko Orgininski...or *Andy Kane*. Get the idea? A short, easy to pronounce name is an asset in the real estate business.

If you are just getting started and not depending on past acquaintances (like sports or entertainment figures usually do), I would suggest shortening your name. Many movie actors and recording stars do this for the simple reason that they want fans to remember their name—Tom Jones, Bob Hope, Fabian, etc. Of course, there are exceptions to everything. Some crazy guy named Dorsey changed his name to Engelbert Humperdink and did quite well, but I would suggest keeping it short and informal if you want to attract clients.

Let's take Zigfried Hennersdorfer. A good version would be Zig Hener. How about Dimko Orgininski? Try Jim Ski. Many potential clients will not call someone with an unusual name for fear of offending them with a mispronunciation. If a client does call on a home listed by Mr. Ditrinco or Mr. Yungkurth, he will not ask for either lister by name for fear of having a tongue spasm or doing serious harm to the ear

13

of the person who answers the phone. It will go something like this:

"Hello, this is Able Homebuyer and I'm calling about the Cape Cod on Nice Street that has your sign in front of it."

"Yes, that's one of our newer listings. My name is Dan Good and I can give you all the details on this listing. It's a three-bedroom at just $91,700. I have floor duty right now but I could show it to you at 4 P.M. today."

"Fine, Mr. Good, I'll meet you there."

Mr. Yungkurth had probably spent considerable time getting this listing; maybe wined and dined the owners, did a comparative market analysis or two, consulted with the owner's son, made various trips to the property, spent time on the phone, prepared a fact sheet, and scheduled advertising. Because his name was as long as a freight train, however, the potential buyer *did not ask for him*! The salesperson who was on duty took the ball and ran, as he should have. If Yungkurth had shortened his handle to Young, he would have had Able Homebuyer's call referred to him and would have been both lister and seller on this transaction.

By retaining some portion of your family name, you will probably prevent your great grandmother's heart failure.

When you announce that you have decided to change your name from Alexander Tomanovich to Al Tomas because you are going into the real estate business, you should also explain that if you retain your name in its present form, the company real estate signs will have to be redesigned to be six inches wider, and your business cards will have to be 2″×5″ instead of 2″×3½″, so they wouldn't fit in anyone's wallet. You will also have to pay for an extra line of type on every classified ad, and that's big bucks. They will understand. So keep it short and sweet.

What's my real name? Andy Kane. I think my parents planned for me to go into real estate or acting when I was born!

THE LUNCH BOX CAPER

As I mentioned before, being distinctive in appearance or custom will help clients remember you. I had an unusual event take place without my planning that created an unusual impression which lasted many years.

Since I have many apartments and listings, it is common for me to have in my possession thirty to forty sets of keys. I kept the keys in a cigar box on my front seat, which became pretty well worn. One day as I was casing a house by attending a garage sale, I spotted a kid's cartoon lunch box—the kind a second grader would take to school with pride. It was metal, just a little bigger than my cigar box, and painted yellow with big-eared mice on it. I paid the fantastic sum of five cents and transferred my stock of keys to the lunch box.

Several weeks later, I was driving a new client around from one property to another. I distinctly remember that the client closely observed my lunch box when I moved it to the back seat, although he did not say anything about it. I happened to have an engagement for lunch that day, so when the client asked if I wanted to stop somewhere for a bite, I replied that I had other plans.

Several weeks later, an acquaintance of this client, who was also a friend of mine, asked if it was really true that I carried my lunch to work in a Mickey Mouse lunch bucket! I chuckled and let it slide, but the rumor persisted for many years, and to this day someone will still mention it.

How To Become Famous

While we are on the subject of your name, let's go off on a tangent on another important subject. No one will remember your name unless they hear it and see it often! Just imagine if the athlete you most admire called you today and asked if you were interested in selling your house. Now imagine that John Doe, Real Estate Salesman, whom you never heard of, called and asked the same question. Obviously, the person with the well-known name will be better received.

You should make a definite attempt to keep your name before the citizens in your area. It must be done periodically, because people have short memories. I have found twice a year is adequate for my purposes. Each year I devise a method to place my name, *which is also the name of my company*, on the front page of the local papers.

Obviously, you can't just walk into a newspaper office and mention that you are in the real estate business and would like your name and/or photo on the front page.

You have to do something newsworthy. The Hillside Strangler, Jack the Ripper, Sirhan-Sirhan, Lee Harvey Oswald, and Son of Sam, all killers, had no trouble at all getting their names on page one, but had they gone into the real estate business, they would not have attracted many clients. You must do something legal, nothing too controversial, and preferably something to help your fellow man.

Let me go over a few of the newsworthy events I have created over the past years. All of them produced new clients immediately and kept my name a household word in the area.

Let's start by analyzing how news gets to the paper. Clark Kent and Lois Lane are no longer with the *Daily Planet*, so we have to rule out supernatural powers. What does that leave? *Tips!* Every paper has a city desk that is a clearinghouse for tips. As information is called or sent in, it is assigned to a reporter to follow up. If there is a certain reporter or columnist who specializes in human or community interest events, you should direct your release or tip directly to him or her. Most feature writers or columnists have to fill a certain amount of column inches each week, and if there is any substance to your tip, they will be happy to use it.

I have had my name or my company's name in a front page story thirty-one times in the last fifteen years, so I'm right about on target for once every six months. Here are a few of the items:

1. *The "water in the basement" problem.* I sold a home to a client and, after the first rainstorm, his basement became wet. He called, and since I knew he had a sense of humor, I immediately sent him a snorkel and diving mask. I did not send it to his house where he would open it in the privacy of his living room. I sent it to him at work, where the joke would be exposed to his fellow employees. If each of the ten guys he works with tells ten friends about the gift "Andy Kane, the Realtor" sent Jim O'Brien, I have reached one hundred potential clients already. I also sent a photo of the items and a copy of the letter that accompanied them to a local humor columnist, and that resulted in a front page article.

2. *Hanover Houses.* The local housing authority owned a project consisting of seven 7-story concrete apartment buildings, which were less than twenty-five years old. The

TIMES-UNION

PETER B.
TAUB

□

Realtor **Andy Kane** says he's willing to go to any lengths — or, in this case, depths — to follow up on the sale of a house.

One of Kane's recent clients was **Jim O'Brien**, a truck salesman at Hallman's Central Chevrolet, who bought a house on Wilsonia Road. A few days later, O'Brien told Kane there was water in the basement.

Kane responded by having a snorkel and diving mask delivered to O'Brien.

"I called him and asked for flippers, too," O'Brien said. And he said his 15-year-old daughter, **Mary**, also wants a snorkel and mask so she'll be "properly equipped" in case she has to go down to the basement.

How much water is there?

"I don't think there's enough to fill a shot glass," O'Brien said.

□

project was known as Hanover Houses and was possibly the most violent housing project in the area. During riots, snipers used the building's roofs as a base. Crime, dope, prostitution, and muggings were everyday affairs. The solution arrived at by the Housing Authority was to tear these buildings down. There was over $5 million owed on it, and it was only twenty-three years old.

At that time I did not own a single masonry building. In fact, the newest and best property I owned was eighty years old and made of wood! I just could not imagine demolishing a concrete housing project that had four-hundred units and was younger than me!

I visited the property and found some things that could be improved. The project had central heat and took a tractor trailer tanker full of oil *a day* to heat during cold weather. To get the farthest building warm, the heat had to be cranked up sky-high! The closest buildings then turned into ovens and those tenants compensated by opening all the windows. I dare say the area immediately surrounding Hanover was about 10 percent warmer than the rest of the city. By installing individual electric heat, with each unit having a thermostat, the costs of heat could be controlled.

One thing that was surprising was that many tenants *liked* living there and did not want to move. All in all, even in its worst condition, it would have been my best property. I estimated that it would cost half a million to tear it down. I made an offer to buy the property for about $1 million. I also sent a copy of the offer to the reporter who had written the original demolition story. This reporter did an in-depth interview with me, the tenants, and the Housing Authority, and the story appeared on page one of the local morning newspaper. The next day, the evening newspaper printed a follow-up story, again on page one.

These stories resulted in two major lenders contacting me to offer funding for acquisition and renovation, and although I was not successful in obtaining Hanover, the investors did finance other properties for me. The local television station also had a question and answer call-in program on the future of the project that featured me, the president of the Hanover Tenant's Association, and other community leaders. The articles in the papers, the TV show, and numerous radio news reports provided an untold amount of free advertisement for my company.

Almost three years passed before an actual decision to demolish the structure was made. There was hardly a soul I met during that time that did not ask me how Hanover was coming. When the final decision was reached, I thought about the money the Housing Authority would have to spend to demolish the building. I made one final offer—not for $1 million, not for $100,000 not for $50,000, but for one measly buck! I again sent a copy of the offer to the media and, low and behold, another front page story!

This renewed exposure three years after the initial affair resulted in many new listings from people who owned investment property and many new buyers who noticed I dealt in investment property.

ROCHESTER, N.Y., WEDNESDAY, DECEMBER 24, 1975

Realtor offers to take over Hanover units

By MICHAEL ZEIGLER

A Rochester real estate agent wants to take financially troubled Hanover House off the city's hands.

Realtor Andy Kane said yesterday he wants to buy the low-income housing project, fix it up and try to make a profit from it.

The Rochester Housing Authority, which owns the project, will respond to Kane's offer, said Thomas F. McHugh, the authority's executive director.

But McHugh said he doesn't see much chance for the idea.

Hanover Houses, a 392-unit project at Joseph Avenue and Herman Street, has lost money since 1969. The city has spent about $1.3 million to cover deficits, and a private consultant has suggested fixing up the 23-year-old complex, tearing down part of it, or tearing down all of it.

Kane said he has plans to fix up each of the seven high-rise towers, but keep them for low-income residents.

One tower would be reserved for singles and would include amenities such as a swimming pool, a gym and a sauna.

He'd like to put a night club, a soul food restaurant, a coffee shop and a temporary job placement center on the ground floor of the towers, he said.

Residents of Hanover Houses have been told they'll be moved to different apartments in the spring, no matter what happens to the buildings.

But Kane thinks he can fix up the buildings one floor at a time, causing residents to be moved only temporarily to new quarters in the same building.

He also thinks he can make a profit. "If you take into consideration the fact that the people who manage this project now get paid every week regardless of whether they collect rents or keep it in operating condition, that shows private management can do better," he said.

A private company would be motivated to collect rents on time and keep the buildings in good shape, he said, because it would be losing money if it didn't.

Kane and the housing authority haven't discussed money or terms. But Kane said if he bought Hanover Houses, he'd expect a property tax exemption until the project began making money.

The Times-Union
Fri., Dec. 26, 1975

Realtor Would Buy Hanover Houses

Realtor Andy Kane said he is convinced the low-income Hanover Houses, which may be demolished, can be made a desirable place to live. He is discussing purchase of Hanover with Rochester Housing Authority Director Thomas McHugh.

Hanover is a 23-year-old housing project which has seven 7-story towers. RHA is operating it at a deficit, and a consultant recommended recently that the project be renovated, demolished or partially demolished.

Kane, who describes himself as a specialist in "distressed" housing, said it would cost the city about $500,000 to demolish the project. Kane said he would

like to buy the project and fix it up and add a night club, restaurant and job placement facility.

Kane said he rents formerly distressed housing in 90 locations in the inner city.

Kane said his willingness to buy Hanover depends on whether or not he can obtain a tax abatement and a suitable disposition of the unpaid $5 million state bond used to finance the project.

McHugh said it is unlikely that Hanover will be sold to Kane.

Two insurance companies already have contacted Kane about financing the renovation of Hanover, Kane said.

...AND THIS IS THE BATHROOM!

Democrat and Chronicle

SATURDAY, OCTOBER 28, 1978

Hanover Houses— $1 offered

By DEDE MURPHY

A Rochester realtor has offered to buy the Hanover Houses from the Rochester Housing Authority for $1 and save the debt-ridden public housing project from demolition once more.

The RHA has asked the U.S. Department of Housing and Urban Development for money to replace the seven high-rise towers with new townhouses. Realtor Andy Kane said yesterday he'd buy the buildings, save the RHA the cost of demoliton, and HUD still could finance the new units.

"It would be a great savings for the RHA and it'd get them out of a headache, too," Kane said.

In a letter to Michael Hanratty, RHA deputy commissioner, Kane said it would cost more than $1 million to knock the buildings down. Instead, he proposed buying the buildings, renovating them and renting them — but they wouldn't be rent subsidized housing units anymore.

Hanratty said yesterday he couldn't comment on Kane's proposal. Kane also offered to buy Hanover Houses in 1975 when the RHA first proposed demolition. At that time, Kane said he offered about $1 million for the project.

"I offered money then because I thought others would want to buy it, too. But no one else wanted it, so I won't make a money offer again," he said.

Two years ago, Hanover Houses was rescued from demolition by HUD's offer to buy the 25-year-old project if the RHA would renovate it. HUD said it would pay about the same price the RHA will have to pay to fix the buildings up — an estimated $19 million.

But, recently HUD suggested money may be available for building new structures and demolition of the project. The RHA board voted to apply for the new construction funds.

---

3. *Andy and the Pope.* It's nice if all your press is related to real estate, but if that's not possible, the next best thing is to get your name before the public some other way. After the Pope visited the United States in 1987, I was at the State Fair. A novelty photo booth had large size cutouts of the President and the Pope. For five bucks you could have your photo taken with either illustrious leader. Great idea!

The story gives the impression I was with the Pope. Read closely and you will see that I never said I met the Pope. The caption just indicates who was in the picture. After this piece ran, I must have had a hundred people ask me what the Pope was really like. I told them he was a real nice guy but he dressed sort of funny!

4. *Acquisition.* A broker who used to work for me started his own company. He operated on a shoestring for a while, then

THE POPE'S VISIT . . .

Pope John Paul II, Realtor Andy Kane

On His Recent 10 Day Visit To The United States, The Pope Met With Many Religious And Business Leaders. The General Consensus Was That There Is Little Chance The Church Will Change Its Stand On Major Issues In The Near Future. If You Are Considering Making A Change In Your Housing In The Near Future, Call ANDY KANE REALTY, 482-3200.

decided to come back to work for me. I purchased his company for a dollar (the same buck I had hanging around that I did not use to buy the Hanover Project). Things were slow, so I made up a press release stating exactly what had occurred, took a few photos, and dropped them off to the media. It let all of the broker's past customers know where he now was. It also created the impression that I had purchased a large company, even though it was a one-man operation, and again my company name was before the public.

The Daily Record, Wednesday, December 2, 1987

COMPANY ACQUIRED: Realtor Andy Kane, right, poses with Vincenzo Cilino, following official ceremony in which Kane, who does business at 1942 E. Main St., acquired VCR Real Estate Brokerage of Webster from Cilino, a licensed broker, and former owner of VCR. He will join the marketing staff of Andy Kane Realty. The acquisition brings the sales and support staff at Kane's to 53 persons. Recruiting of 10 additional salespeople is under way, he said.

5. *The answer is short skirts*! Several months had passed since I attracted any media exposure for my company, so in the spring of 1979, during the gas crunch, I proposed a solution to the problem.

6. *Current events.* When the Iranians took a few American hostages in the late 1970s, I had T-shirts printed up with the suggestion that an obscene act be committed on Iran. Underneath read, "compliments of Andy Kane Realty." The shirts were a big hit and made local television. The cameraman was cautious not to offend the viewers. The two people who were on camera were asked to each block out one of the letters in the first word. One held his hand over the "F" on his shirt and the other held his over the "K." The viewers got the message and my shirts got national attention.

Democrat and Chronicle

Opinion Page

8A   TUESDAY, MARCH 27, 1979

To save energy, shorten skirts

THE PRESENT long length of women's skirts is a waste of energy. Many of the materials used in today's fabrics are made using petroleum by-products. By reducing the length of skirts to half of their present length, a 50 percent savings of these oil by-products would be possible.

Since sewing these skirts would require less time, a savings in electricity required to power sewing machines and illuminate work areas is realized.

Making skirts half as long would increase production by 100 percent, since only half much time will be required for manufacturing. This will better utilize the assorted energy sources required to heat and light the skirt factory.

The cartons used to pack these skirts need only be half as large as cartons used to pack present ones. This will save great amounts of energy used in production and shipping of empty cartons to the skirt factory. It will also conserve the trees in our forests, which would have become paper pulp for the larger boxes.

The skirts, when boxed, will take only half as much space in trucks used to transport them to the department store, thus eliminating one truck and the accompanying fuel and oil consumption.

The skirts, when displayed for sale, will not require as much space and more can be displayed in the same space required for today's long skirts. This means more efficient use of the heating and cooling systems in the store, since we now have twice as much product available in the same space.

My rough calculations indicate that the energy saved in the entire process mentioned above would possibly be as much as 1½ percent of our nation's energy requirement. Since this represents approximately the same amount as we were receiving from Iran, it is my belief that by switching to shorter skirts, we alleviate the pending energy shortage.

Every patriotic energy-conscious woman who is contemplating a new wardrobe should insist on shorter skirts!

ANDY KANE, 1942 East Main St.

7. *Reference books.* Reference books are published for just about every category imaginable. If you have the opportunity to be solicited for information (the publisher must request information; you don't just volunteer to be in the next edition), it is worthwhile to take the time to fill in any forms or supply any data that is requested. Approximately one person in twenty thousand is invited to submit their information. (*Who's Who* is copyrighted by Vulcan Publications.)

Some of the other media coverage of my company are shown here. Get to work and come up with some interesting events to promote yourself!

Who'sWho

KANE, ANDY, real estate broker and developer, writer, consultant; b. Rochester, N.Y., Oct. 1, 1936; s. Edwin M. and Marie A. (Carroll) K.; m. Evelyn F. Martin, Aug. 30, 1965; children—Colleen, Glenn. Student Rochester Inst. Tech., 1954-60. Cert. appraiser Nat. Assn. Realtors, 1979. Race car driver NASCAR, Daytona Beach, Fla., 1954-65; pres., chief exec. officer Andy Kane Engring., Greece, N.Y., 1954-78; pres., chief exec. officer Allstate Mktg., Rochester, N.Y., 1977-80; pres., chief exec. officer Andy Kane Realty Corp., Rochester, 1967—; pres. East Main Realty, Rochester, 1978—, also dir.; dir. Nat. Energy Inst., Rochester, 1980—. Author: Care of Tenants, 1980, Revenge of Tenants, 1982, Saloon Survival, 1984, How to Double Your Money, 1983. Named Kiwanian of the Yr., Kiwanis, 1979. Mem. Internat. Orgn. Real Estate Appraisors, N.Y. State Assn. Realtors, Nat. Assn. Realtors, U.S. C. of C., Am. Entrepenpreneurs Assn. Republican. Roman Catholic. Lodges: Moose, Kiwanis. Avocations: writing; radio talk show guest; auto racing. Home: 149 Crosman

Terr Rochester NY 14630 Office: Andy Kane Realty Kane Office Bldg Suite 400 1942 Main St Rochester NY 14609

21st edition
1986-1987

Andy Kane Realty At Spencer Speedway 8/26

WILLIAMSON, NY...As preparations begin to make the track ready for the 1988 season, Speedway officials are pleased to announce is the return of Andy Kane Realty on Friday, August 26th.

Andy Kane Realty is a large local real estate company that handles commercial residential and property management and rentals. The addition of this sponsor will mean bonus monies for both the Late Models and Super Stocks. In addition the feature winners will receive special trophies from Andy Kane.

Realty Firm Has 'em Buggy

First there was Ripoff Construction, an enterprise described in this space a few weeks ago.

Now we have Cockroach Realty, which, like Ripoff Construction, showed up in The Daily Record under new corporations.

The owner is **Andy Kane**, a real estate broker who deals in inner-city rental property. Friends kidded him by referring to his business as Cockroach Realty, and then tenants picked up the joke and began making out checks that way.

"When I recorded the name at the county clerk's office, the girls there tried to talk me out of using it," Kane said. "They thought it would be bad for my business."

Like all new businesses, Cockroach Realty has gotten a lot of form-letter sales pitches, many of them with handwritten notes asking if that's really the name of a real estate company.

* * *

PETER B. TAUB

Think of it as touch of class

The well-preserved city: Andy Kane Realty is boosting next year's sesquicentennial with T-shirts that say: "Happy 150th Birthday Rochester ... You Don't Look a Day Over 90!"

☐

UPSTATE UPDATE

MALE SUPREMACIST LANDLORD

From his picture and what he has to say, you're sure that he must have a gruff and gravelly voice. How else would you expect a man who writes books with titles such as *The Care and Feeding of Tenants* and *Mastering the Art of Male Supremacy* to sound?

But no, he has almost a sweet voice. Does he really believe that tenants should be treated like children and that women should be kept in line? Is it all a put-on?

"Nah, it's just me. I don't really worry about how I come across to other people," says Andy Kane, owner of Andy Kane Realty, Allstate Rentals and Main Street East Rochester Realty. As well as being author of the above books, he has written *Saloon Survival* and *Jobs that Suck . . . and Some That Don't.*

Andy Kane

But Kane, 51, says he wasn't always able to say what he wanted. That's when he worked for others, like Xerox, when it was Haloid, and Eastman Kodak Co. He had one of those, well, less than desirable jobs. And then in the 1960s he found one that was just plain fun for him — real estate. He owns about 170 apartment units, manages more than 200 units, and owns the above businesses at 1942 E. Main St.

Kane, who lives in Penfield, is enjoying the fruits of his labor. His two grown children and a son-in-law now work for him. That means he can take vacations. Five years ago he took his first vacation. And every year he adds a week. "It keeps me from fighting with the tenants."

Kane has been married to his wife, Evelyn, for "25 long, hard years." He says he's managed it by being away a lot. But going on vacation with her "is the only time I get close to murdering her. That happens when you're around someone that much. And I always make the decisions about where we're going to go and what we're going to do. That's the man's job."

By year's end, Kane will have yet another tome published. It will be a handbook for real estate agents telling what he's learned over the years. But he won't reveal the title or details of the contents. "It's a very unusual title. A real kicker."

— Charles Derlang

Your Appearance

Now that we have knocked your name around, let's attack your appearance. You will have to deal with all types of people when you list a home. You are going to represent them and they know it. If you are a male with a pierced ear and a peace sign hanging around your neck, or a female with the biggest boobs on earth and a dress cut down to your belly button, you might make it in certain fields but I don't think you will in real estate. You must look neat when you meet your potential lister. In the words of the famous Rocky Simeone, "You only get one chance to make a first impression." Your appearance should be either casual or dressy, depending on the circumstances, but it should always be neat.

I have found out that custom-tailored suits cost only a little more than those off the plain pipe racks. My haberdasher, Abe Supporta, takes great pride in his work. He requests that you return for free alterations if you gain or lose weight so that the fit will be complimentary to his work. I have never worn one of Abe's suits without someone complimenting me on it. The cost is about $100 more per suit.

I can assure you the tailors at the store with the plain pipe racks don't give a damn how you look—they are just putting in their forty hours. When was the last time someone asked you where you got your suit? Find a good haberdasher and use him. Be sure to leave a supply of your cards with him as well. (How do you find a good haberdasher in your area? Ask the best-dressed men.)

Everyone wants a successful person selling their home. If you look successful, you will attract clients. Show-business people are experts at "putting up a front," the show business term for looking prosperous, even if you are broke.

We have had a couple of presidents who cavorted around the White House in jeans. It raised the standards of jeans to new heights. If you feel comfortable in jeans (nice dressy jeans, not a pair with a patch on the ass), you might try wearing them to an appointment with certain clients who are "with it."

You should appear to conform to local styles if you are going to attract customers. If you are in the Midwest and earrings are not popular on males, you should avoid them. If you are in Los Angeles, you may want to get your ear pierced. If you are in a locale where ties are unheard of, go with the flow. If you can function properly and are acceptable to your clients in a bathing suit, golf shorts, or any other attire, that's the way to go. Of course, you cannot dress regally and forget to shave!

Your hair should also be in style. Shoulder length or a ponytail on guys looks good if you are a guitarist with a heavy metal band, but may well turn off a buyer if you are selling a home.

Bald? Heaven forbid that you consider a wig! I have *never* seen a good one. Bald is fine, since it lends distinction to your appearance. Remember the old saying, "God only made so many perfect heads. . .the rest He covered with hair!" My brother-in-law sells real estate and he decided to invest in a wig a few years ago. It looked like a beaver was sleeping on top of his head! My insurance man also has a "rug." While he was taking riding lessons, his wig flew off! It looked so much like an animal that the barn cat attacked it!

My advice; instead of a wig, spend the money on a good

psychiatrist who can help you overcome your fear of having a shiny dome! I find that many clients who encounter a salesman with a wig back off and go to someone else who they feel is more confident in his appearance and abilities and does not need a piece of fake hair to build up his courage.

You probably have also seen the used-car salesman wearing a plaid or polka dot coat or a ten-gallon Stetson hat. It makes him easy to find on the car lot, and it works. Maybe you can devise an outfit that makes you stand out without looking ridiculous. Give it a try.

Being comfortable is the key. If lawyers and bankers are really comfortable in those three-piece blue suits, why don't they wear them on Saturday? When they are out of the office and prowling around the house, the suit is in the closet and the jeans are covering their fat fannies!

Your Car

Your car is another extension of you, so it should indicate success. It should be a late model and bright color so people will see you around town and know you are active. Red, white, yellow, or green all stand out. A Cadillac—even one that is two or three years old—is still an excellent status symbol and a comfortable car for showing clients around town. Keep it neat, clean, and in good running order. If you are driving a rusty six-year-old car when you drive up for a listing, you have two strikes against you before you knock on the door.

When I traded my three-year-old Ford in and started driving a new Cadillac Eldorado, my sales doubled in three months! So buy a late model luxury car, even if you have to starve the wife and kids.

A few years ago, a salesman in a company that I worked for analyzed my secret of a good tailored suit and a sharp car. He had been working for the company two years longer than I and was doing about 10 percent of what I was doing in sales. Joe went out and bought a nice, new, off-the-rack suit and a three-year-old dark brown Cadillac. Is Joe a top producer today? No. He is operating a cleaning business for restaurants. The off-the-rack suit fit like an off-the-rack suit, and you couldn't find that dark brown Cadillac in traffic if it had a police flasher on the roof!

You should also rent, lease, or buy a car phone. This is not a luxury anymore, *it is a necessity.* You can save hours with a car phone. You will impress your clients and increase your efficiency in both listing and selling. If your selling area is rural, you may want to include a CB radio in your selling tools.

Many states offer vanity or personalized plates for your car. If you are well known in your area, these plates can be a great advertising gimmick. Since my name and company name are the same, I have an ad on my bumper 365 days a year. Many potential listers will have you look at their home, but they do not want the neighbors to know they are selling. They call and say, "Don't walk around the outside. Don't take any pictures. Don't talk to my neightbors," and so on, and I respect their wishes. I do, however, park my bright red Cadillac Eldorado with the license plates "ANDY KANE" in the most prominent place I can find. I park either in their driveway partially over the sidewalk, so it is conspicuous, or right in front of the house about a foot and a half from the curb, so it is noticeable. After I go, the neighbors usually call the potential lister and say, "Are you selling? I saw Andy Kane,

the real estate guy, at your house!" This demonstrates to the potential lister that I am well known in the business, which reinforces their confidence in listing with me.

Keep good records of your auto expenses, mileage, use for personal business, and related expenses, such as insurance, tags, parking, car washes, etc., so that you can claim every tax deduction you are entitled to.

THE "ASS FOR EVERY SEAT" CAPER

While we are on the subject of cars, let me tell you what the car dealers say when they get a real dog on their used car lot. They say, "There is an ass for every seat!" This means that no matter how bad a car is, there is someone who will come along and fall in love with it. The same is true for houses. If you try hard enough, you will find a buyer. I personally have *never* turned down a listing, no matter how bad it was. I firmly believe that I have listed the worst property in the world.

One of these listings was a filthy Cape Cod in an average part of town. The owner was running from the law for desertion from the military. The house was so filthy, your feet stuck to the floor. The smell was unbearable. Every flat surface—tabletops, mantle, counters—had cans, ashtrays, dirty dishes, and cat shit on it. I had to take the owner out to the hood of my car to sign the listing because I could not find a clean spot in the house on which to lay it down. I posted a sign out front and hoped no one would call to see it.

The next day I got a live one. I explained it needed a bit of cleaning, but they were undaunted. I met them at the property and tried to go inside, but the foul air gagged me. I pretended to have a cough, put my hand over my mouth to cover the gagging, and went back outside to throw up. The buyers stayed inside for about ten minutes, then came out looking like they had just seen the best house in town. When they said they wanted to put an offer in on it, I could hardly believe it. I had found an ass for my seat!

Business Card Tricks For Fun and Profit

You have all seen magicians perform card tricks. You can do card tricks that will pay off better than Harry Houdini's! I give away hundreds of business cards per week, thousands per year, and it really pays off.

First and foremost, your card should be distinct. How many salesmen's cards have you thrown away that looked cheap? Regular black printing on a plain white card, flimsy stock—cheap from the word go! I always think of a funeral director when I get one of those cheap black and white cards.

Like your car, your card is an extension of you, and it should reflect you. It should stand out when thrown on a table with other cards. At a recent real estate seminar, Ray Hunter, the speaker, collected cards from all of the 250 salesmen in attendance and picked one at random. You guessed it—it was my card! My card is not gaudy. It contains the name of my company, my office and home phone numbers, my photo, and the realtor logo. It is printed on white glossy stock with red raised thermographic lettering. It is regular business card size—no folds or unusual size.

A card like mine breaks the ice when you hand it to some-one. They always look at the photo and make a comment:

you look better (or worse) in person, you look older or younger, or what have you! I always tell them I had it retouched, or my friend, Burt Reynolds, stood in for me, or something like that so they remember me.

Another reason to have your photo is retention of cards. When someone gives you their photo, you don't throw it out. That is just not done. Look around your home. I bet you have your brother-in-law's ugliest kid's picture on your mantle—I do. You just can't throw away someone's picture.

Another good reason to put your photo on your card is because many people see you every day. They may not remember your name, but they will know your mug! When they see your card with your photo, they identify you with it, and you are more likely to get their listing.

Have you noticed the wanted posters in the post office? Once a criminal has his photo hanging there, he is seriously hampered from doing business, or even going out in daylight. Your photo will work the opposite for you. When your card is received by an old acquaintance through the mail, or from a mutual friend, that old acquaintance may not remember your name, but your pretty face—how could he forget that!

I actually use several different cards to suit different circumstances. I have some with a wide-brim black hat that I give out in places such as rock or country bars and concerts, and to anyone who I feel would enjoy a unique card. It's sort of a "bad guy" card. I also have cards that have a large color photo with me holding a white, good-guy hat and a split-level family-type home in the background.

Use caution when selecting outfits to use in your photo, because if you are wearing a leisure suit or Nehru jacket, your card will be in style only as long as those items of clothing are in style. I have many other cards with other photos so I can fit the card to the occasion.

Now that we have the style of card out of the way, let's get into the tricks.

You have hundreds of opportunities each day to distribute your cards in unique ways. Every time you send a letter, pay a bill by mail, send a greeting card of any type (Christmas,

ANDY KANE REALTY
1942 MAIN STREET EAST
ROCHESTER, N.Y. 14609

OFFICE:
(716) 482-3200
RESIDENCE:
REALTOR® **(716) 442-0181**

ANDY KANE
REALTOR, AUTHOR
APPRAISER

ANDY KANE REALTY
SALES • APPRAISALS • MORTGAGES • RENTALS
1942 East Main Street • Rochester, New York 14609

ANDY KANE
Realtor — Author — Appraiser

OFFICE: (716) 482-3200
RESIDENCE: (716) 248-3177

birthday, get well, etc.), include your card! Even if it's your car or mortgage payment that you send to the bank every month, put your card in it. Although that envelope always goes to the same bank, the chances of the same person opening it each month are remote, and it may get you a listing. You say you send your mortgage payment to a mortgage banker three thousand miles away? Put your card in it! In this day of corporate relocation, you never know when you are going to get a call from someone three thousand miles away who just found out he was being transferred from the main office to the branch in your area.

Never leave your home or office without carrying a supply of business cards. Place a supply in your car and give them to the attendant when you buy gas. Give them to toll collectors, parking lot attendants, traffic cops, hookers, and anyone else you come in contact with while on the road. I have purposely deflated one of my rear tires slightly to attract attention. When someone would come up to me as I parked and say, "I think your tire is going flat!" I would say, "Thank you very much. I have an important real estate deal in a few minutes and if I missed it, I could lose thousands!" I then hand them my card and say, "If you are ever in the market for real estate, give me a call and I will return the favor."

This trick does two things: 1) it impresses them that you are involved in "important" real estate deals, even though your biggest sale so far has been a dog house; and 2) it creates the illusion that if they call you for real estate, you will save them "thousands" like they saved for you by telling you about the soft tire. I have used the soft tire trick for years with great success. I have even had people come into my office and ask who owned the red Cadillac Eldorado, and then tell me about the soft tire. I have also ruined a tire or two, but that put me in contact with the tire store—and I sold the house that was owned by the guy who changed my tires!

When you have lunch, leave your card with the tip. Be sure the tip is not too big, or the waiter or waitress may think you don't need the business, and not too small, or they may think you're a cheap S.O.B.

When you use a pay phone, leave your card as a bookmark in the phone book. (If no one is looking, rip out the entire real estate section, and leave your card there!) This is especially important in airports. I never pass the airport without stopping in and placing several of my cards in all the telephone booths.

Visit apartment houses for senior citizens. Contact the manager and leave some of your cards. Mention that if any referrals are received from this manager, you would like to take him or her out to dinner. Most senior citizen housing that is subsidized requires the applicants to sell their homes before they may reside there. You will be doing both the manager and the applicant a favor by listing the home.

Visit attorney's offices and leave your card. They have many opportunities to send a listing your way. When you have a client who does not have an attorney, you can refer him to the attorney who sends you a listing.

Even in the most ridiculous places you should have that card handy. When you go to the beach and are clad only in a bathing suit, you should have cards in your beach bag. I have listed many properties and made many valuable contacts at the beach. I can think of no place on Earth where the opportunity could not arise to pass out your card.

If you keep it a secret that you are in the real estate business, you will not last very long. Make a list right now of the places you should leave a supply of your cards. I will start the list to jog your mind into action:

1. *Undertakers*: As ghoulish as this sounds, the funeral director assists the family in purchasing a grave site, casket, and in making many other decisions. If he gives them your card, they may very well list the deceased person's home with you.

2. *Barber shop*: Have you ever noticed that barbers never stop talking? Get him to talk about real estate and hand out your cards. Beauty shops are also in this category.

3. *Your minister or priest*: Many times they are in a position to send you a listing. A parishioner usually tells him when they are planning to leave the parish. Be sure to make a large

contribution to the church—$50 or $100 when you get this listing sold and I guarantee that you will get many more!

4. *Your doctor*: Elderly people moving to nursing homes, death, handicapped individuals moving to more convenient homes, heart attack victims who must sell a two-story to avoid stairs, etc. Your doctor comes in contact with all of them.

5. *Personnel Departments*: People are in and out of these places all day, moving out of town or to different divisions.

6. *Bankers, loan companies, insurance agents, fire adjustors*: You can and should continue this list until you have at least ten more places you can drop your cards. Be sure to reward every bird dog who sends you a lead with a bottle of liquor, box of candy, dinner, or something, so they know you appreciate the referral. It will pay off in continued referrals.

These cards may not produce immediate results, but I consider them to be time bombs. You never know when they are going to go off. I have had clients call two, three, even four years after they received my card.

Wrong Way Corrigan

What would happen if you drove the wrong way on a one-way street? Just visualize it for a moment; cars dodging you for the whole length of the street. How many cars going the

right way noticed you? All of them, of course. If you were going the right way, only two would have noticed you—the one in front and the one in back.

The next time you enter a supermarket, use this technique. This market may have five hundred potential listers walking the aisles—friends, neighbors, old school buddies, etc. If you fall in with the general pattern, only the one ahead of you and the one behind will see you. The other 498 won't even know you are in the store.

Along the same line, when you grab your shopping cart and everyone is headed for the produce section on the east end of the store, you head for the baked goods section at the west end. You then will meet face-to-face everyone who is in the store and all who enter after you. This will give you the greatest exposure to potential customers. If you would have gone through the store in the normal manner, a potential lister may have been two old ladies and three cans of beans ahead of you, and you never would have met them. Be sure you have a supply of business cards with you.

Prospecting: Finding Real Estate Listings

Listings are the backbone of the real estate industry. The more listings you have, the greater your yearly income will be. If you have ever gone out to buy a new or used car, I am sure you went to the dealer with the greatest selection to choose from.

The same thing is true in the real estate business. The office with the most listings attracts the most buyers. The salesman with the most listings will be the most successful!

In this chapter, I will tell you some of the unusual methods to obtain listings. Unusual, but practical. I can assure you that I have obtained listings using all of these techniques. Some of these will result in an immediate listing, while others will produce contacts who will later list or buy.

Let me start with your daily routine. Full- or part-time salesmen all have one thing in common. They get out of bed each morning when the alarm clock goes off and they go to their places of business.

I want you to get a pencil and paper and write down each major thing you do from the time the alarm rings until you reach your office, including the streets that you use on the way to the office. Stop now, and write everything down.

People are creatures of habit, and what I am going to tell you will make it necessary to break some habits, but it will also result in many new listings. On your paper you have probably written something like this: get out of bed, take shower, dress, eat breakfast, read paper, get in car, drive down Pine Street to Oak Street, etc. This is absolutely the wrong answer. Let me show you a plan to make 125 new acquaintances and enlist the aid of five new bird dogs. (A bird dog, by the way, is someone who is around when you are not and passes out your business cards.)

Here we go, step-by-step, from the alarm. Get out of bed, take a shower, get dressed—every day is the same *until here!* Now, get an area map and lay out five *different* routes to the office. Use side streets, roundabout routes, inconvenient routes, and so on. Each route should contain a small coffee shop, restaurant, or donut shop. No large ones, just places big enough to accommodate about twenty-five people. Mark the five routes Monday through Friday.

Each day, take a different route and stop at the coffee shop or restaurant. Sit at the counter where a conversation is most likely to occur. (Tables are not conducive to making acquaintances.) Case the joint the first two weeks—keep an eye out for the owner, who will usually work the cash register or cook. Bring your paper and read it while having coffee. Leave a tip, and say "Good morning" when entering and "Have a nice day" when you leave.

The third week, you go into action. Without standing up and shouting that you are in the real estate business and you are here to sell each of them a house, make it known that you are in the real estate business. There are many ways to do this, and I will give you just a few.

The Phantom Call

Usually a pay phone will be available within earshot of the customers. Call your wife, time and temperature, or any other useless number. Put your finger in your ear, so that it appears you are having a difficult time conversing with the party on the other end, and speak slightly loud. Take a purchase offer out of your pocket and carry on a conversation something like this: "This is Andy Kane, Realtor, calling. The seller accepted your counteroffer last night, Mr. Thomas. It was quite late, so I didn't call you then. I will make all the arrangements for a mortgage today, and you should be in your new home in thirty days." Everyone within range of your voice will now know who their new realtor is!

The statement I used is designed to subconsciously get across several points. Let's take it apart:

"It was late, so I didn't call you then." This indicates you have consideration for the client. You didn't call at 1:30 A.M. from a local bar and holler, "Hey, you just bought a house! Aren't you happy?" You waited, like a professional, until a reasonable time to inform the customer.

"I will make the arrangements for a mortgage today." By this you have indicated that you can arrange financing. This is important to both buyer and seller. Most clients have no idea how to arrange financing and they will rely on you to obtain it.

"You should be in your new home in thirty days" indicates you can rapidly arrange and process all the documents and transfer title to the new buyers without unnecessary delay. We use the word *home* in this statement because we are talking to a buyer. Home creates a desire. Home is an important thing. It's warm, cozy, and secure. It is just what the buyer is looking for: a home.

Never refer to it as a "house" when you are talking to a buyer. House is impersonal. House is a structure, just a bunch of sticks and bricks. A house is easily parted with. A home is very important; a house is not! When you show your clients a property they appear to like, refer to that property from then on as a home. After you call this property "home" several times, the clients are mentally going to refer to this as home themselves. Once they have "moved" mentally into this home, it will be easy to get their signatures on a purchase offer!

The exact opposite is true when you go to list a property. Never call it a home, call it a house. When you refer to it as a home, you increase the seller's attachment to the property. It's hard for him to part with a home; it's easy to part with a house! When you say "home," you bring back memories: past Christmases, the son born in the east bedroom, Grandma's last Thanksgiving in the dining room, the kids' heights marked on the dining room door frame, etc. So call it a house! The street is full of houses—they are just sticks and bricks...no memories.

Never forget—it's a "home" when you talk to a buyer; it's a "house" when you talk to a seller.

A Voice In Your Pocket

Many salesmen carry pocket voice pagers. If you have one, try this. Turn the volume up all the way and arrange for your wife to call you at the exact time you are at the restaurant. Prepare a script for her to use, like this: "Mr. Kane, this is the office. The owners have accepted the offer on Clearview Drive. They would like you to find them a new residence in the Glenwood area as soon as possible." Incidentally, you just happen to be in the Glenwood Coffee Shop! You can be sure that any of the twenty-five customers in the coffee shop who are considering selling their homes will not let you out the door when you finish your coffee.

The Newspaper Ploy

Open to the want ads. Find the ad for your most recent listing, nudge the guy on the stool next to you, point to the ad and say: "If I had ten more like this one, I could sell them all today. I sold this one last night, and I had ten more calls after I got home." Give him your card.

Setting Up The Bird Dog

The first thing you must do is compliment the owner on his food and how nice he keeps his place. Even if the food is terrible, compliment him on how good it is. You can buy a lot of Rolaids with that commission check!

All small-business men hate government paperwork. This is a good way to start up a conversation. Mention that you are really bogged down with government paperwork or tax forms, and you bet he has the same problems. He will immediately ask what business you are in (if he has not already heard the pager or the phone call). Gain his confidence by mentioning all the property you are selling in his area, and indicate that you are very successful in the real estate business. Ask him if you can leave a few of your cards on the counter, near the register. He can't refuse. . .you like his rotten food! Mention that when a lead develops from his restaurant you will take him and his wife out to dinner. He can sample someone else's cooking! You have now established your bird dog operation. Do this at each place you eat and you have five bird dogs in your corner.

The Pay Phone Ad

Most pay phones have a picture-frame bracket on front that contains dialing instructions for long distance and other information. Using a nail file or knife, gently pull back the top center of the frame and drop your business card inside so it will be visible to every user of this phone. The card will usually stay there for a long time and be seen by hundreds of people before some phone man takes the time to remove it.

Be A Bird Watcher

One of the advantages of using a different route each day is that you will notice the FSBOs! An FSBO is the rare bird who tries to sell his own home—FOR SALE BY OWNER. Your various routes will take you by five times as many homes each day as the old route did. Be sure you contact every FSBO. Don't assume that he will be uncooperative or has been contacted by twelve salesmen already. Most FSBOs become discouraged and eventually list.

Make his acquaintance and offer assistance in the sale. Check back every ten days to see how he is doing. If you have someone in your car, stop out front and gesture toward his shack. Make believe this hitchhiker is a client. Try to be noticed pulling up—screech the brakes or get out and slam a few doors. He will call you.

Little Old Ladies

They are in season in early spring and summer. You will see them raking and maintaining their property. Stop and tell them how nice their yard looks and how you notice it each time you go by. Compliments mean a lot to them, just like they did to the cook. Tell them you could get a buyer in a minute for a home with a yard like this. Mention that the cost of maintaining a house must be really high, with taxes and utilities what they are. If there are any subsidized rental units for the elderly, mention this also. Offer to obtain any information you can on renting one of these units. Most rent for a small percentage of their income, a fact that most elderly people are unaware of. This could result in a savings of thousands of dollars over owning a home. You may not list this home today, but you are planting a seed in their mind. Keep calling or dropping them a note. You *will* list it!

All of these techniques are effective in building listings. Just by changing a few of your early morning habits, you have increased your exposure to available FSBOs, made 125 new acquaintances at five coffee shops, obtained five bird dogs...and it isn't even nine o'clock in the morning yet!

I have used and still use all of these methods. They have accounted for hundreds of thousands of dollars worth of new listings for me.

Well, now we have made it to the office. It does not matter whether you are at the real estate office or another office. You are going to meet people today. I would like to quote two famous remarks, and you should try to memorize both.

The first one is by Don Hutson, the famous real estate speaker: "Contacts breed contracts." The more people you come in contact with, the more chances you have to obtain a listing contract.

The second was conveyed to me by Joe Girard, "the Greatest Salesman in the World," as proclaimed by the *Guinness Book of World Records* for several years. It is called the "Girard Law of 250."

Joe visited the funeral parlors in the Detroit area to pay

his last respects to departed clients. At each funeral parlor, he noticed prayer cards with the deceased's date of birth and death and a prayer. He realized that the funeral director had to order a certain number of cards, and he set about to discover how the director knew how many to print. He interviewed many directors and found that almost all had 250 cards printed! After years of experience, they had discovered that most ordinary working stiffs of the middle class had 250 friends that appeared at the funeral parlor.

That means that every person you meet today, even those middle-class working stiffs that you and I deal with in listing real estate, has 250 friends who he will tell what a good real estate man you are (or, if he is dissatisfied, what a bad real estate man you are). The 250 people are all potential listers.

So the more people you meet the better your chances are of obtaining a listing ("contacts breed contracts"). You better do your best to satisfy each one, because if you do, that one could result in 250 referrals or, if he is not satisfied, could eliminate a possible 250 clients ("the Girard Law of 250").

Let me get into some of the techniques you can use to increase your exposure to potential listers.

Using A "Shill" To Get Listings

Here is a way to make some money when it's a slow day and everybody is dogging it. You will notice many salesmen congregate in groups to tell war stories and swap excuses—the listings they *almost* got last night, how the weather is too bad to go out and knock on the door, or even how the weather is too good to go out prospecting. All this will not put one dollar in your pocket, but this trick will!

Stay away from these salesmen. You don't need them. They certainly aren't going to list anything with you. Your time is better spent looking for listings. While they are having coffee and you are presently not with a client, grab the Criss-Cross directory that lists streets, residents, and phone numbers. Find an area that was settled thirty to forty years ago. These areas were generally populated with people who were in their twenties then, who have had time to bring up their kids, get them married, and now have a four-bedroom house for just the two of them. Call each one of them and use the following technique.

Introduce yourself, then begin: "Mr. Davis, I was in your neighborhood with a client yesterday looking for homes for sale. My client jotted down your address and asked me to check to see if you may be considering selling."

If you get *any* response, be ready to go over today and visit the property. When the owner asks where your client is, tell him you will bring him over as soon as the listing is signed. Are you wondering where you will get this client? As unprofessional as it sounds, you are going to use a "shill."

A shill is a person who is not really interested, but will appear to be. A fake. A Stooge. You get the idea. You will see them at auctions when the bidding is low. He is working for the owner and he will be bidding to get the price up. At a carnival, he will be walking around with a big expensive teddy bear, telling how he won it for a quarter at the "pitch till you win" booth. Your shill will be serving the same purpose, but he will be different.

Carefully pick a friend who will accompany you to look at the potential listing. Let him know the entire scheme. Tell him you will buy him a drink, or coffee, or something like that, right after looking at the house. One more thing...*be sure your friend is qualified to buy a home.* Apartment dwellers are excellent candidates.

After you take him through the potential listing, tell him you have to stop at the office and jot down some information while the property is fresh in your mind (and also fresh in his mind). Immediately sit down and figure out down payment and monthly mortgage payments for the property. Compare this with the shill's monthly rent. Discuss appreciation and equity, tax advantages, and other benefits, and you may very well have sold this listing already!

How To Double Your Listings

When you go over to a client's home to list the property, have certain information already typed on the listing: the address, assessment, lot size, owner's name and phone number, and anything else that is obtainable in advance. Also, *type* in the date the listing begins and the date it expires. This term should be twice the length of time that listings are usually taken for!

I have used this technique for years and seldom had a complaint from any clients. If the client does notice the dates when signing, you can save face and retain the client's confidence by saying, "The secretary in the office typed this for me. Most of our clients list for six months to give us adequate advertising time." The client may very well not change it after hearing this, or he may ask you to reduce it to three months, which you can easily do with the stroke of a pen!

A Bonus

While we are on the subject of listing contracts, let's discuss the rate of commission. Let's say the rate charged by most realtors in my area is 6 percent. The United States Government has seen fit to decide that all commission rates are negotiable between sellers and brokers. This is good for you. If the property is not an easily salable property (ghetto, poor shape, slobs living there, etc.), you should charge a higher commission, something like 8 percent or even 10 percent. You can explain that this property will take more advertising and much more effort to sell than a suburban property, and for this reason you must charge a higher rate. The difference between 6 percent and 10 percent on several transactions will increase your income by thousands of dollars each year.

I have also found that you may even get more than the standard 6 percent to sell a good listing. In my area, the sales tax on most purchases is 7 percent. People get really used to seeing 7 percent on everything they buy. Many times I drop a 7 percent instead of 6 percent on a listing contract and it does not even raise an eyebrow, since the locals see the 7 percent so often. Give it a try. Now, aren't you glad you bought this book!

HOW I LEARNED TO SPEAK POLISH CAPER

Several years ago, I listed a home in a predominant Polish neighborhood. I received a call from a Polish gentleman who had recently arrived in the United States from a communist country. He was a well-qualified buyer who was employed by a large Philharmonic Orchestra as an associate conductor. He spoke fluent English and we prepared a purchase offer. The offer was accepted and I scheduled an appointment with the bank for a mortgage application.

I told the buyer some of the information the bank would require: past address, nearest relative, past employment, etc. He replied, "I have family back in the old country. I give no information!" Not wanting to lose a deal, I came up with this plan. I would take his wife to the bank. She spoke not one word of English. I told her husband to tell her that whenever I looked at her and spoke gibberish, she was to say six or seven words back to me in Polish.

When we arrived at the appointment, I explained to the loan officer that I would interpret the necessary questions. The loan officer asked what the buyer's husband earned. I looked at the buyer's wife and mumbled some gibberish. She looked at me and said something in Polish. I turned to the loan officer and said, "$68,000 a year." "What kind of car do you own?" Gibberish, gibberish, Volkswagon, etc., back and forth until the application was completed. They got the mortgage, I got my commission, and I can add being an interpreter to my list of past jobs.

Organizations

By all means, join professional organizations such as the Society of Real Estate Appraisers, Real Estate Board committees, and the like. Unfortunately, the only contacts you will make here are other people looking for listings—no buyers or sellers!

Join civic and service organizations such as the Lions, Eagles, Kiwanis, Knights of Columbus, Masons, etc. Use caution in joining, however. Your main interest is helping Number One, so scout the organizations carefully to discover if other real estate salesmen are in the group. If they are, try another organization. You are bound to find one where you will be the only one. Then it will be like shooting fish in a barrel. I personally visited the Lions and Eagles before deciding on the Downtown Kiwanis Club. Most service clubs frown on soliciting fellow members for personal gain, so you must use some unusual techniques to do business.

After I had been a member of the Kiwanis for about a month, I donated a sum of money to their handicapped children's fund. I did this at the weekly meeting with the statement that a member of the club had referred a listing to me, and it is my policy to reward any organization that refers a client to me. This indeed *had not* occurred, but it was a way to bring to the members' attention the fact that I would donate to the club's favorite charity when business was sent my way. Two weeks later, an attorney who was a member referred a brick, two-family listing to me, and the following week an elder club member called upon me to list his home. Remember to keep making donations after each sale. If things are slow, create another "phantom" sale to start the ball rolling again.

Operating two real estate companies occupies much of my time, so I am limited in the number of service organizations that I can belong to. If you are a salesman, you should seriously consider joining more than one community organization. Avoid political parties, however. They can hurt you because only one party wins. If you are strongly identified with the loser, you lose also.

Generally speaking, this process will work in just about *any* organization, even if the organization is not one that ranks

high in the respect of the community (Communist Party, Ku Klux Klan, Nazi Party, etc.). Members will help other members if they can. If you already are a member in good standing of some lunatic fringe group, don't be afraid to solicit business from your fellow lunatic lodge brothers.

Be careful that your efforts do not get out of control in your endeavor to assist the crippled kids or crazies. Many times people get carried away with duties to the organization and forget their main goal. . .helping yourself! I had one salesman who eventually devoted all his free time to the endeavors of the club and *stopped selling real estate!* He even used his vacation time to work on club projects instead of taking his family to the mountains. The tail wagged the dog!

Service organizations are there for *your* benefit. *Help Number One;* it's the American way. God Bless America!

THE "WE GOT THE MONEY" CAPER

A visiting Kiwanian who resided in Tennessee wanted to sell a house in Rochester, New York, my area of operation. I listed it and advertised the place, and a young couple in their thirties responded. I showed them the place and we sat down to write a purchase offer.

They had an old junk car, dirty clothes, smelly little kids, and very few teeth. I asked them how they would finance this house, which was very cheap for the area because the owner wanted out fast. They replied that they would have the money for a cash deal. Doubting that they had seventy-five cents in their filthy jeans, I asked if they had this money right now. Answer: No. . .but they would have it shortly. I explained that if they made a cash offer and it was accepted and they could not come up with the cash, they could be liable in a court case for nonperformance on a contract. They said they understood perfectly and there would be "no problem with the cash." I asked if this windfall was from an accident settlement, inheritance, or a gift from a parent. Answer: No. . .but they really did not want to divulge the source.

Okay, I present the offer and it gets accepted; we are ready to close. I contact the buyers and they tell me they need a "little more time" to get the cash. I say no problem but only if I know where the cash is coming from. They finally tell me.

A large fast food chain was offering a million dollars if you could spell out F.A.S.T. B.E.R.G.E.R. with little coupons! They were spending eight to ten hours a day going from one Fastberger joint to another, buying one cheap item to get another coupon. I ended up buying the house myself to keep from being sued for incompetency by the seller.

I later read that there were ten million of every letter in circulation with the exception of the B. There were three of them in the entire universe!

Moral of the story: Be sure the buyer has what he says he has!

Referrals

Again, I would like to tell you of a technique used by Joe Girard, "The Greatest Salesman in the World" according to the *Guinness Book of World Records*. Joe keeps a book with the name of each client he has ever dealt with and his birthday. On the birthday, Joe sends the customer a birthday card with his business card inside. He indicated how much value he places on his client birthday book by regularly having it copied and the copies placed in a safe-deposit box!

Long ago I began using a book to list all of my clients. This book has proven its usefulness many times. I do not send out birthday cards, but I send out thank-you cards such as the ones you would receive after a wedding. In fact, I had them printed by a wedding invitation printer!

When you get home after a hard day's work, I am sure you don't read every piece of junk mail. You probably look at the return address—Reader's Digest Sweepstakes, ABC Vacuum Cleaners, etc.—and promptly file them unopened in the trash. My thank-you card comes in an envelope exactly like a wedding invitation, only without a return address. The card is engraved as a wedding invitation would be, with the following note: "Thank you for allowing me to be of service to you in past real estate transactions. If you or any of your friends are considering buying or selling, I would be happy to give your transaction my personal attention. Sincerely, Andy Kane." I enclose three of my business cards.

The thank-you cards are never sent at holidays or otherwise busy times and never on the first of the month. They are usually mailed to arrive on a Tuesday or Wednesday to give the most exposure and time for a client to read it. If it arrives with other mail, your effort may take a backseat to the client's interest in his pension check or bills.

Does this system work? Every mailing I have ever made, and there have been many, has produced at least one new listing. Even at the present postage rate, that new listing is worth the expense.

More Referrals

When a client lists with you, ask him if he knows of anyone else in the area who is thinking of selling. Neighbors, especially older ones, know a lot about what is going on in their area. Many oldsters belong to senior citizen clubs or organizations. Try to arrange to attend one of their meetings and answer any real estate questions they may have. Important things older people want to know about selling their properties are: how much tax will they have to pay on the gain; on the average, how long is property listed before a sale; what are area values; points on FHA/VA mortgages; how long after a sale will they have to be out of their house. Be prepared with all the answers.

When they ask about value, offer to do a free market-value analysis of their property. Even if they are not selling in the near future, the analysis will be beneficial to them for insurance purposes. Often when a person has owned a home for a long time, the insured value is way below market value and a fire could wipe out any equity that inflation has built up.

By doing an analysis of the property, you get a chance to visit the prospective listers personally and in their own home. Be especially observant. When you see photos on the mantel stop and look at each one. Ask who this lovely child is. "Oh, that's my granddaughter, and this one is the son who moved to Arizona," and so forth.

Now you know that Mr. and Mrs. Oldtimer are living in this five-bedroom home all alone. "How much did it cost to heat the big house last year? I see from the assessor that your taxes are $1,000 a year. Insurance has skyrocketed in the past few years, hasn't it Mr. and Mrs. Oldtimer? How much was yours? It looks like we have a total of $3,000 for fixed expenses on this big house, not counting repairs and maintenance. Even though you own it free and clear, you have an enormous expense for just two people. Plymouth Gardens, the senior citizen complex, has apartments for as little as $150 a month, and that includes utilities. That's $1,800 a year, or a saving of $1,200 over your fixed expenses. If you sold this house for $80,000 and put that in the bank at 8 percent interest, you would receive over $6,400 in interest alone. That would pay your rent and give you enough to fly to Arizona to see your son at Christmas!"

Now you've got them thinking. Never try to use high pressure to list. You have planted the seed in their minds. That's enough for now. When you send them the written analysis of their property, include the financial data you have discussed. Lay it out, as you would a profit-and-loss statement, so they can study it. Also, include a brochure from the senior citizen's complex and any other information about the complex you may have obtained, such as bingo nights, craft workshops, etc. You have laid the groundwork; now just give them some time and you will have the listing.

Mark the calendar to send them a follow-up letter in sixty days, and add their name to your potential client list.

THE WRONG HOUSE CAPER

I sent out some thank-you's to past clients. One resulted in a call from Florida from a client who wanted to sell his two-family house "at the corner of Jefferson Avenue and Hawley Street." I was familiar with the area, although I had not sold him this particular property, but we agreed upon a price. I drove over to the corner of Jefferson and Hawley and hung a sign on the property, which was vacant, vandalized, and did not have a house number on it.

Within days I had an offer from an investor who did renovations. I called the client and the offer was accepted. Before the transfer of title, I received another call about this property. It was from the owner, who had driven by and noticed my sign on his property! I had assumed the Florida client's house was at the corner of Jefferson and Hawley, but it was actually at number 932, *one* house from the corner. The house I put the sign on was number 934.

I asked the owner of 934 if he would be interested in selling for the price I had already gotten and he agreed! That's not the end. Number 932 was really better than 934, and if the investor was willing to pay x amount for 934, he certainly would pay that for 932. He was, and I sold both!

I wouldn't suggest putting the sign on the wrong house too many times, but in this case, it worked out for the best.

Appointments

Two or more people agree to meet at a predetermined location at a prearranged time. Sounds simple, but you would be amazed at the number of times you will be at 149 Crosman Terrace at exactly 2 P.M. and your buyer will be waiting in your office across town! Appointments are the backbone of the real estate industry. You will have to deal with scheduling daily appointments if you are to succeed in this racket.

Let's go over some appointments and their circumstances. Let's say you are into golf, boating, beaches, or bimbos. You want to take off Wednesday afternoon. You do not want to tell potential clients that you are going to tie one on, or they may lose confidence in you. When your home buyer wants to see a shack on Wednesday at 2 P.M., you simply tell him that it would be better to wait until Thursday morning because you are listing a property on Wednesday afternoon that you are sure will be of interest to him.

Always be sure all concerned agree on the time and place of the appointment. If the client is new to you, ask what he will be wearing, driving, or what he looks like. Describe yourself and your Cadillac or Mercedes. Be sure the client understands he is meeting you at the property for sale and not your office. Be on time or early. I personally arrive ten or fifteen minutes before the appointed time and look around to familiarize myself with the property. It's also an opportunity to give your card out and introduce yourself to the neighbors. They are potential listers and you may hear from them.

Now a potential lister calls. People will live in a home for sixty, seventy, or eighty years! When they decide to sell it and call you, you must go immediately! Do not ever delay an appointment with a potential lister. If you tell them you are busy this afternoon and cannot make it until this evening at 7 P.M. they will call someone else. Go immediately to any potential listing, even if you have to rearrange your golf game or miss a kickoff. Let the client pick a time. When a client calls to see a property, I ask "When would be good for you?" This shows some consideration for their time. If they pick a time when I already have an appointment, I just tell them, "I have one at 10. How about 11?"

Piggyback

Many clients need a little prodding to make a decision to buy. One good way to get them to jump is to create an atmosphere of urgency. You make two appointments about one hour apart to show the same property to two prospective buyers. Be sure to delay the first buyer until you see the second buyer drive up. This will create the impression that there is much interest in the property and it will not be available long. It will usually increase the amount of the initial offer, since each buyer will assume the other is making a good offer on the property.

The Appointment You Never Make

You just got an offer for 26 Elm Street. It's for $106,000 and the asking price is $111,900. If you personally call the sellers, what will be the first thing they ask? "How much is it for?" When you tell them, they will say "Don't even come over," or "No way." Even if they don't say that, they will have time to find excuses why they cannot take $106,000 before you even arrive. The easiest way to alleviate this problem is not to talk to the sellers! Have your secretary or wife or some third party call the sellers and say, "Andy has a *very good* offer on your house and he will be there at 10 A.M. to present it." When you arrive, the feeling will be positive. They are expecting a *very good* offer and they have not had time to build up any resentment. It works every time.

THE DRAGNET CAPER

Some agents think distressed property is hard to sell. Not true! I have sold many properties that were distressed in one way or another. One particular property was real hard to show because the tenants refused to cooperate whenever I tried to make an appointment to inspect it.

The owner was a client who had inherited some rooming houses from his mother. One Saturday morning, after a wild Friday night, two of the tenants got into a donnybrook and one ended up dead. The client called to tell me, "Get an offer today. I want out!"

I got in touch with a potential buyer—a friend of mine, who could handle most any type of tenant—and he met me at the property. He and I both had pagers and sidearms on our belts. We stepped over the chalk marks on the porch where the dead body had been and entered the property. Prior to our visit, several detectives and police officers had searched all the tenants in their investigation of the murder.

I always had problems showing this property to prospective purchasers in the past, but on this day all I had to do was knock on each door. The tenants saw our pagers and sidearms and immediately assumed we were more cops. They did not want a hassle, so they let us in immediately, walked over to the wall, and assumed the position you see on TV—hands on the wall, feet on the floor, legs apart! We inspected the place with ease and my friend made an offer that was immediately accepted.

Getting The Offer

Getting the potential buyer to make a formal written offer is the first step in putting that commission money in your pocket. Whether the custom in your area is to write the actual offer in a letter of intent or a memorandum of purchase, you must get a signature on an official document that indicates the price to be paid, how it's to be paid, when transfer will take place, and so forth. Since you are almost always representing the seller, your job is to get the best price on this offer.

For buyers I recommend he make his best offer first. If you have shown him the property in the manner I mentioned in the previous chapter, he knows others are interested in this cave. If the price is $119,900 and that is reasonable for the area, I usually suggest an offer slightly over the asking price, like $120,000. If your buyer balks at paying more than the price, mention that others may make a full price offer and his will upseat that for just a hundred bucks! It may be the difference between getting this cave or having to start looking all over again.

A deposit is a big boost in closing a deal. When the seller sees a check to Andy Kane Realty "as deposit" in the amount of $5,000, he knows he has a real serious buyer. The buyer is also less likely to have "buyer's remorse" and consider backing out if he has some bucks up front.

I have seen many cases of buyer's remorse in my years. Buyer's remorse is caused by second thoughts: Did I pay too much? Could I find a better home for the same price? My brother-in-law thinks I got screwed. You get the idea. You have probably had the same thing happen to you after you made a major purchase. The first thing you saw on your new $4,000, 48-inch, rear projector television was a commercial for the same set at $3,500! That's fate and it should be expected.

Treat the buyer's remorse with respect and explain why the property is a good deal. I have always done this, and still two of my buyers have committed suicide. (Incidently, suicide will not get them out of the deal. The buyer's estate is bound to fulfill any obligations the buyer has made before death. Remind any buyers of this if they threaten to blow their brains out.) I don't feel it was my fault since both had other problems (mental, job, etc.), but you should always keep it in mind that some people cannot handle things as well as others.

I personally like my offers to be a work of art. I either type or carefully print (thanks to ten years as a draftsman) all information. Every detail should be spelled out. Any property or item that could possibly become controversial if removed should be specified as included or not included (such as weather vanes, decorative fountains). A beautiful built-in wet bar with oak top and black leather trim is not much good if the seller takes the ten beautiful oak and black leather bar stools with him! If, when the present owner shows you around, he drools, salivates, or gets overly excited when he shows you the beautiful marble shrine to his patron saint that was built by his great grandfather before he died, beware! This could be considered personal property and removed by the seller, even though it might weigh several tons!

If your buyer wants the shrine, be sure you put it in the offer. If the statuary is gone when the buyer takes possession, you may be liable. The offer should be complete in every detail, including dates, buyer's name, address, attorney's infor-

mation, and any adjustments that are to be made for taxes, fuel, and other items. I have found that the more complete the offer is, the more chance it will be accepted as is. If there are rents, leases, tenants' rights, or other unusual terms, be sure they are covered in full. Any copies of documents detailing terms of lease, options, and so forth, should be made part of the purchase offer. I usually bring an offer that only needs *one more thing* to be complete—the seller's signature under the acceptance paragraph!

There are all types of offers preprinted by stationery companies or devised by real estate companies or real estate boards. You should carefully select the one you feel comfortable with, familiarize yourself with every term, and have your attorney review it to be sure that it conforms to the legal requirements of your state and locale.

THE SALTING THE MINE CAPER

You probably heard of someone selling a dry gold mine by loading a shotgun with gold and firing it into the mine walls. That's salting the mine. A novice sees the gold in the walls and buys the mine. Do you think somebody could salt an apartment building?

A client of mine had a rooming house for sale. Unknown to me, it was 75 percent vacant, although he maintained that it was full. A buyer wanted to see it, so I called Bobby, the owner, to set it up for 9 A.M. the following morning. Bobby owned several topless bars and had some girls at his beck and call.

I arrived with my client, who was a young man, and knocked on room #1. The door opened and Smarty-Pants, one of Bobby's voluptuous dancers attired only in bikini pants, greeted us. She said come in and look around. My client never took his eyes off the girl.

We next knocked on #2. A gruff and growling male voice said he worked nights: "Go away!" (Bobby was in there.) We knocked on #3, but no answer. We tried the door and it was unlocked. A lamp was lit by the bed, a cigarette was burning in the ash tray, and the bathroom door was closed, so tenant #3 must be in the crapper. (Bobby had lit the cigarette before going into #2.)

Number 4 was next. Knock, knock; "Who is it?" (Bobby had run from #2 to #4 while we were in #3.) "Real estate man," I hollered. Response: "I'm just getting ready for work and I'm late. Come back in ten minutes and I'll be gone; I will leave it unlocked." Number 5 was locked and no one home. Number 6—knock, knock; "Come on in." Tenant is still in bed. (Bobby with the covers wrapped around him, face toward the wall.) Numbers 7 and 8—tenants let us in but they were really the only paying tenants in the whole place. At #9, Bobby says from inside that he also is getting ready for work, but will leave the door unlocked, etc.

Out of fourteen units, only two were really rented, but Bobby had convinced us that the place was full! The buyer had one request: "Could I look at #1 again?" I certainly did not mind, and Smarty Pants was happy to oblige.

I sold the building to this guy. Moral of the story: don't believe everything you see in real estate deals.

Presenting The Offer

Your wife, secretary, or girlfriend has set up the appointment for you to present the offer. You walk in, smile, looking like the cat that just swallowed the mouse, and say loud enough for it to be heard on the next block, "Your house is sold!" You do this even if the offer is $5,000 less and they already told you they would break your skull if you brought anything less than a full price, all cash offer! So why do you greet them with, "Your house is sold?" It's psychological! You want them to start thinking *sold*.

You gather around the kitchen table and begin explaining the offer. You do not start with the price. You say, "Mr. and Mrs. Eager Buyer do not have to sell anything to buy your house. There is no contingency regarding sale of other property. They are apartment dwellers. Isn't that good!" Nod your head yes and they will do the same. "They had A-1, ironclad, great credit and should go through the bank like crap through a constipated goose. Isn't that good!" Nod and they nod. "They are making a $15,000 down payment and I have the check right here." (Pass it under their noses so they smell it). "Isn't that good!" Nod and they nod. "The closing date is September 1, the day you requested because you are moving into your new home on Spectacular Avenue. Isn't that great" Nod and they nod. "Their offer is for $155,000."

Immediately swing the offer around to the husband (sorry ladies, that's the custom), take your pen and place the point right on the beginning of the seller acceptance signature line. Tip the pen toward the seller, but don't let go of it. Hold this position without saying one more word. He will either take the pen and sign it or break your skull. Just kidding, but it does work many times.

I have had some memorable presentations. One incident occurred several years ago at my office. I got to the part where I tip the pen toward the seller. He reached out and spread his hand, palm down, in the middle of the offer. He then closed his hand, crumpling the offer into a small ball, threw it in my face, and walked out without saying one word. I guess he did not like the offer.

If they accept the offer, shake their hands and get out of there. Indicate that you will take care of everything from that point on, and then say goodbye.

If They Don't Take The Offer

Give it one more try. Mention that this property has been on the market a zillion days, heavily advertised three hundred cars a day see the sign in front, it has been open for inspection twenty-three weeks in a row, shown to 371 potential buyers, multiple listed (which draws the attention of 915 licensed brokers and salespeople), and this is the first offer! These people are willing to pay $155,000, and a counter may kill the deal by scaring them away. Explain to the sellers, "All you have to do is sign here and your house is sold. You sleep well tonight, and you start packing tomorrow. No more showings in the middle of the afternoon sex matinee or during dinner. Peace of mind will be yours with the stroke of a pen!"

Mention that it is as if their house is on the auction block, and someone likes it and has bid $155,000. They are in effect trying to buy it back for $160,000. That's crazy! Sign here. If all this fails and they insist on writing a counteroffer, try a compromise offer.

Split The Difference

I say, "Look, let's split the difference—$157,500." Most sensible sellers will go along with this. Sit down and write a counteroffer that is good until the next morning. Don't try to complete the deal today. You have already got the buyer to sign an offer for what they considered a good, fair price once today. Don't try twice. Many brokers make this mistake. They will keep everybody up until one in the morning going back and forth like a Ping-Pong ball. It's better to keep the buyer in suspense overnight.

Presenting The Counteroffer

Again, have someone call the buyer and set up an appointment. They should say, "Mr. Home Buyer, Andy would like to stop over at 11 A.M. He has some good news for you." Now you have them thinking positive. They are already moving in their mind. When you come through the door, you smile and say, "They took your offer," pause. . .and in a lower tone of voice, you say "except". . .sit down at the table, get out the offer..."they came down $2,500 from their asking price, instead of the $5,000 we asked them to come down. It's still the best deal in town. The reason they were willing to come down is they must be in their new home by September 1, and that fits your timetable perfectly."

Turn the offer to the husband, place the tip of your pen on the dotted line, and tip the pen toward him. Congratulations! You have an accepted offer! You can now feed the screaming brats at home and pay your mortage for another month.

Obviously, you will have to develop more techniques than just this one. Remember what words and actions get buyers and sellers to sign and reuse the ones that work.

Financing The Shack

In about 80 percent of your sales, you will encounter buyers who just don't have $2,000,000 cash on hand to buy a home. Being quite well-off yourself, you probably can't imagine this, but some people have to float a loan to buy their dream house. If you want this deal to close, you must arrange the financing on the sale. When I started selling real estate, there were four ways to finance a deal:

1. FHA or VA loans with very low down payments.

2. Conventional loans through local banks with about 20 percent down.

3. Assume existing loan and pay difference in cash or second mortgage.

4. Owner financing.

I'll bet you think it was easy in the old days. Unfortunately if one of these four ways didn't work, you had a dead deal. I recently read an article listing over three thousand different methods to finance a home. These three thousand combinations change daily, and if you took the time to learn all of the combinations and terms of these thousands of available financing plans, you should be finished just about in time to collect your first social security check!

So what do you do? Cultivate a few people from the local lending institutions who are knowledgeable and make a living by placing mortages. You should learn the basics and leave the rest to the experts. Know how much down, closing costs, bank fees, loan to value ratio, qualifying factors, and so on. A good loan counselor will be able to better advise your buyer as to what mortgage plan will benefit them for their circumstances. Possibly a low interest, adjustable rate mortgage would be best if the buyer is planning to relocate in three years, or a fixed rate long term if the buyer is going to be in the home for many moons. You will find it best to use one lending institution for all your deals because if you establish a good rapport with them, they will get a deal through that may not have made it otherwise.

You should not lose track of the old faithful "owner holds the mortgage" because this is the easiest and fastest way to sell a home. When you do this, you have a deal and your job is done as soon as the offer is signed. The seller pays your commission from his proceeds, and he gets his payments each month for the next twenty years. No trips to the bank, no waiting for a commitment.

If you are attempting to get a deal through using owner financing, you should present it in the following manner: Carefully figure how much the seller will receive over the life of the mortgage. (Multiply monthly principal and interest times number of months mortgage is to run.) This sum is usually much greater than a straight cash sale, possibly two or three times as much. Explain that should the buyer ever default on the payment, the seller could reclaim the property through foreclosure and resell it. The sale price usually will be higher, since appreciation generally drives up prices every year. All the previous payments are kept by the seller, of course.

Most sellers will immediately ask, "What if something happens to the buyer and he can't pay the monthly payments?" Mention to them that when Andy Kane sells a home and he holds the mortgage, he prays that something happens to the buyer (layoff from job, hit by bus, jailed, etc.), so that he can foreclose and resell the dump to someone else, keeping the down payment and monthly payments. Good luck!

THE PIECES OF SILVER CAPER

Houses may be sold for something other than "normal" currency. Several years ago, a couple of brothers in Texas tried to corner the silver market. The price of silver skyrocketed. An individual who was a numismatist (that's a coin collector to us regular idiots) had a large collection of silver dollars and wanted to buy a house. He converted the going rate for his cartwheels into regular folding bucks (something like one silver dollar for each seven dollars of real money) and make an offer based upon paying silver at the closing.

The seller was ecstatic! His closing statement would show he actually sold his home for a loss. He paid only a real estate commission based upon 6 percent of the silver dollars total. The buyer was happy because he could demand that his tax assessment be based upon the sale price. The transaction was completely legal, since the silver dollars were good old U.S. currency. The seller held on to the cartwheels until the price went even higher. Then he took his pile down to a coin dealer and cashed in really big!

Open House

I hate open houses. In my part of the country (Great Lakes area), you schedule an open house, call the paper, place the ad on Wednesday or Thursday in good weather, and have three feet of snow on Sunday. You can end up walking back and forth in the living room talking to yourself.

Open houses are usually held because the seller does not think you are doing enough to sell his shack. Since the seller does not know that you are telling five buyers a day about his overpriced hovel and distributing information to other cooperating brokers, he assumes you are not working hard enough for him. If you hold it open Sunday, he *knows* you are working on his sale.

There are, however, several good reasons to hold an open house. Some of them are:

1. *Prospects:* If someone climbs over the snowbanks and comes in, he is probably a reasonably serious buyer. He obviously is interested in a house this size, in this area of town, and in this price range. If this particular property does not fit his needs, you can find another property that does.

2. *Exposure:* The neighbors see you holding this shack open and realize that you are active in the area. They may later list with you because of this open house.

Planning An Open House

Contrary to what many real estate people think, open houses do not just happen. They require planning, just like a Broadway play.

The difference is you, Cecil B. DeSalesman, are going to direct and produce this extravaganza at 53 Park Avenue. First, set the stage: Tell Joe Homeowner that you want the house to be spotless, yard cut or snow shoveled, kids' rooms clean, toilet flushed, closets in order, cat litter out, and he and the family gone from noon to 6 P.M. on Sunday. You are holding an open house from 1 to 5, but he should leave early and not come back until the crowd leaves so he does not get in the way.

Next, check out the neighborhood, especially the homes immediately to the right, left, and across the street. If you find anything that may disturb a buyer (such as a family with eight unruly, screaming brats, fanatics or cult creatures who might hold a demonstration or religious service, or drunks, crazies, druggies, or other types that may turn a buyer off), let me suggest this:

Call the offending neighbors and say: "This is station WRKP. Your name has been selected by the computer to receive tickets to Sunday's baseball (football, soccer, wrestling, dog fight, etc.) game. How many tickets will you need? Eleven? Fine, we will get them in the mail today."

On Sunday your neighborhood misfits will be sitting happily on the fifty-yard line, swilling suds, while you are writing a purchase offer on that nice, quiet home at 53 Park Avenue.

The next step is to insure a good crowd for the opening. Don't bother putting an ad in the theater section; the classifieds will do. Contrary to the general opinion of other real estate professionals, the ad should be detailed and give the *price*. Many real estate people think that an ad should be vague so they can get leads. That is not true. Many people will simply not show up if they don't know what the price is.

The ad should be descriptive enough to attract a buyer. Keep in mind you will be spending a nice Sunday afternoon sitting in this place. Your ad should be big enough to attract

BEACHWOOD AREA: 132 Par-
sells. Open 1-3 today. com-
oletely renovated. 8 rm Victorian.
new kitchen. 2 baths. new gas
heat. gar. taxes just $656. This 5
bdrm home only $30,900. Mtg
avail. Andy Kane Realty 482-
3200. 442-0181.

potential buyers or you will be wasting your time.

If the street is not a familiar one, give the area in the ad so it can be easily found. Anything out of the ordinary should be mentioned in the ad. You would be surprised how many people buy a home just because it has a skylight, dog run, hot tub, or some other attractive item. If the taxes are low for the area, be sure it is mentioned. If they are high, forget it. Your phone number is important. Someone may read your ad and have a date with his mistress between 1 and 5 on Sunday. If your phone number is in the ad, he can then call you for a private showing at 5:30 or noon. You don't want to lose any potential buyers for lack of a phone number.

Increasing Traffic

As director of this extravaganza, you should do everything in your power to increase the number of visitors to your open house. If the Goodyear blimp is available, you should use it, but since it is probably covering a football game somewhere, you will have to use other methods.

One of the most important, little known facts in real estate is, "Who would buy this house?" If you know exactly who, your job is obviously made very easy. I know who. It is someone with ties to the neighborhood, such as:

1. A friend or working associate of the neighbor.
2. A relative (especially a son or daughter) of a neighbor.
3. Someone who works in the neighborhood or travels through the area on his way to work.

The reasons are many. They can ride back and forth to the mines with Charlie and save a buck or two on gas. The mother-in-law can baby-sit. They won't have as far a drive to work.

Now that you know this deep dark secret, you just have to grab these individuals and pull them into your open house. The easiest way to let the neighbors know that this dream house is on the market is to use a postcard.

Arrive about an hour early. Let the owner know that you are going to be canvassing the neighborhood for possible leads to buyers for his home. This will make him feel good, and he may even inform you of a neighbor who has grown children who are renters.

Go to each home on the street and say that you have the property at 50 Brett Road for sale and it is open today. If they know of any friends, co-workers, or relatives looking to move, they could give them a call and inform them of the property. You will give these people your personal attention. Do this even though you have already mailed cards to these same people.

When you show people through this lovely property, keep in mind one thing. *Do not say;* "And this is the bathroom!"

Note: Use caution when having an open house in urban areas where crime is a good possibility. The following tips may be of some help:

1. Take along a buddy, like that new kid in the office who could use the experience, or another salesperson to share the leads with.

2. Keep an eye on the visitors to be sure they do not pocket the silverware. Keep a log and have them sign it, and jot down their license numbers.

3. Many burglars use an open house to case the place, noting valuables, windows, alarms, etc. Some will unlock a window or garage door for later entry. If the client seems more interested in doors, windows, paintings, and furnishings, instead of price, taxes, and annual utility bills, keep an eye on him.

4. Leave your purse in the trunk of your car, not on a table where one potential buyer can distract you while another grabs your money, credit cards, and keys.

I don't want anything to happen to you, unless of course you sell real estate in Rochester, New York. Then I wouldn't mind if the competition gets eliminated so that my salespeople will have it a little easier.

Qualifying The Buyer

There are many ways of qualifying a buyer. There are formulas and equations: x percent of gross income, x percent of net after fixed expenses, x percent of annual income determines the price of the home, etc. These are all nice handy yardsticks to use, but they have one bad thing in common: They *dis*qualify many buyers!

My method of qualifying a buyer is:

1. Take your right hand and using your thumb and first finger...

2. lightly grasp the buyer's left wrist. Your thumb should be on the outside of his wrist, your finger on the inside.

3. If you feel a slight throbbing (also called a pulse), the buyer is unequivocally, irrevocably, eminently, 100 percent qualified to buy a house!

This method works well for me. Many times I have taken clients that were discarded by other real estate offices and sold that "unqualified" client a home.

The trick is to use creative financing. If the client is not eligible for bank financing due to excessive debts and obligations, he can still buy a home if:

1. He has something of value for a down payment (money,

motorcycle, boat, video games).

2. He has some regular income (welfare, stealing, counterfeiting, dealing dope, etc.).

3. You can find an owner who is anxious to sell and will hold the mortgage with another owner, who will hold a second mortgage.

If this guy, who is a black sheep, walks into the office at the same time as good-as-gold Joe with the eight-to-five job and five grand for a down payment, I always put the black sheep on the back burner and work with the well-qualified buyer first. That's just common sense. When you have a slow day, you call up the black sheep and fill in your time with him.

I admit it is harder to find a home for the unqualified buyer, but I have done it hundreds of times.

Down Payments

Most novice and even some experienced real estate people think of a down payment as cash and cash only. If a buyer is lacking a cash down payment, many real estate pros give him the fast shuffle and that's it!

They lose many sales this way. You should be a detective. If he does not have cash, see what else he may have.

Some examples of down payments include boats, motor

homes, coin collections, guns, antiques, securities, bonds, jewelry, computers, and tools. Some of these items may not bring top buck at present, such as a boat in the winter, snowmobile in July, stock when the market is down, wife while pregnant, etc., but they all have future value.

Tell the seller that the buyer will give him the $5,000 cruiser as a down payment. The seller can hang on to it until spring and possibly sell it for $7,000. If the seller doesn't want a boat, the buyer can sell his cruiser at a loss for $4,500 right now and use the funds for the downstroke.

You must suggest the maneuvers to the buyer. Use logic. Ask him, "Why keep the boat you only use twelve weekends a year when the funds can get you a home 365 days a year?"

Many times you will encounter a seller who does not want to accept a race horse, antique car, beer can collection, or similar fantastically valuable items as a down payment in place of cold hard cash. What do you do next? Figure out the sum of your commission. The part of the down payment earmarked for your commission could possibly be equal to the value of the item offered. Consider accepting the item in lieu of payment for your services. It makes the deal, and you can always keep, use, or sell the item later.

If it is something dangerous (wild animal), expensive to keep (fat wife), or functionally obsolete (last year's home computer), you can always give it to someone you don't like as a Christmas gift.

The point is, nearly everyone is qualified and has a down payment of some type. You just have to work a little harder to put a deal together. Remember, adding sales to "unqualified" buyers to your annual sales may just make you the top dog in your office.

Once you get the unqualified buyer into a shack, don't ignore him. Stay in contact, because usually a client of this caliber has friends of similar virtues. "Birds of a feather, flock together." When his friends see that the guy they steal hubcaps with bought a house, they will all want one! You have a ready-made stream of "unqualified buyers" to whom you can sell houses when things are slow.

If he has a housewarming and you get invited, be sure to attend and bring plenty of business cards!

Buyer's Requirements

One of the first things the average real estate salesperson does when a buyer comes into his office is to sit down and discuss the buyer's requirements for a home. He usually gets a piece of paper and a pen and writes down these very, very important requirements:

- Attached, 2½-car garage with automatic door opener.
- Doghouse with fenced-in dog run big enough for male German shepherd.
- Walking distance (2-3 blocks maximum) to health spa so fat wife can work out.
- At least four bedrooms (they only have one stinkin' kid) so they can have overnight guests twice a year.
- At least three full bathrooms and one powder room (in case they all have to go at exactly the same time).
- Laundry room on first floor so fat wife won't have to walk downstairs.
- Close to day-care center so the brats won't be underfoot.
- Fireplace in family room, raised hearth, oak mantel if possible because hubby's high school basketball trophy looks good on oak mantel.

If you are one of the thousands of salespeople who do this,

let me tell you what your next step should be. Assuming that you have compiled this very, very valuable information on an 8½-by-11-inch piece of paper, carefully follow these instructions:

1. Fold the paper in half, lengthwise.
2. Carefully fold each half diagonally from the center front to the opposite corner. You now will have a V-shaped fold.
3. Now fold each half once again from the point to halfway up the opposite side.

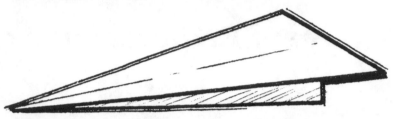

4. Gently twist the point to secure the folds.
5. Grasp the bottom center with your right hand and throw. Measure the distance the paper plane travels. If you go over one hundred-seven feet four inches, you have the world's record for indoor flight.

I think by now you have gotten the idea. Never pay attention to the buyer's requirements. You are a professionally trained real estate person. You should decide, based on logical information (area, price, family size), what is suitable for them. If you were a doctor, would you allow your patients to write their own prescriptions? Certainly not. I use a 3"×5" card and record only the pertinent information I feel is necessary to select properties to show.

When you take the buyer out to view the homes you have chosen and they say, "But it doesn't have a doghouse" (or electric garage door opener, or an oak mantel on the fireplace) your answer will be, "I realized that when I selected this home, but since this property is priced at what I consider several thousand dollars below market value, I didn't want to rule it out because of a $97 item."

You should never argue with the buyer over his requirements or objections. You should overcome each objection with

NAME Jim Cook	☑BUY ☐ RENT	
ADDRESS 1934 East ST	DATE 1-17	
	HOME PHONE 482-3274	
BUS ADDRESS Temple Products (CULVER)	BUS PHONE 516-3500 (4-12 pm)	
NO OF CHILDREN 2	AGES OF GIRLS 5	AGES OF BOYS 11
CASH DOWN 7-8000.	PRICE RANGE 75,—	MONTHLY PAYMENTS 900	GI	FHA	CONV 1
TYPE OF HOUSE DESIRED RANCH - CITY	ROOMS NEEDED 6	BATHS NEEDED 1 1/2	BEDROOMS NEEDED 3
SPECIAL REQUIREMENTS (LOCATION DESIRED ETC) EASTER PART OF COUNTY —		
PRESENT HOME ☑OWN? ☐ RENT?	INCOME 55/	OCCUPATION PROD ENGINEER
HEARD OF US FROM RADIO AD - WROK		SALESMAN DON PEZOR

common sense and factual, logical answers, such as:

Objection: "But it only has three bedrooms and when my mother comes from Sticksville, Pennsylvania, for Christmas, where will she sleep?"

Answer: "The cost of a four-bedroom home in this tract is about $8,000 more than this model. That is a lot of money for a bedroom used once a year. How about using some of that savings to buy a nice sofa for the family room that converts to a double bed?" Or maybe even "There is a nice Holiday Inn only a mile away. Your mother would love staying there once a year. It would also make it a little vacation for her."

Objection: The wife says, "It's nearly a mile to the Body Beautiful health spa?"

Answers: "Look fatso. . ." No, you better not use that! Try, "My wife found that walking the extra block or so to the spa was sort of a warm-up for her exercises." I then flip out my wallet with a photo of my wife in her bikini and say, "I think the walking really helped her." The buyer's fat wife will immediately have visions of her pounds melting away as she drags her body the two miles to the spa. (If your wife is fat, use a photo of your girlfriend, cut one out of a girlie magazine, or send me $2 and I will send you a picture of my wife.)

Buyer's requirements are really like that of a kid who makes out a three-page wish-list for Santa. He doesn't really expect all the items, and he usually is satisfied with only one or two on Christmas morning.

Don't fall into the trap of trying to come up with this ideal home the buyer has described, because it doesn't exist. If you do (and I did years ago), you will be searching the computerized multiple listings, calling other brokers, and scanning the classifieds for a week. When you finally find the home that has 99 percent of the buyer's required features and you call your buyer, the conversation will probably go something like this:

"Hi, Mr. Buyer, this is Sam, super salesman, from Dream Home Realty. I found what I think is the perfect. . .What? . . .You have *already* purchased a home?"

After he left your office last Sunday leaving his wish-list for you to work on (four-bedroom Cape Cod on lower east side, two-car heated garage), he passed an open house on the upper north side, a two-bedroom ranch with a carport, and fell in love with it.

At this point, many salesmen clean out their desks, turn in their licenses, and get jobs on the assembly line at the local sweatshop packing film in little yellow boxes or screwing left lug nuts on new Chevrolets.

"I Dunno"

For many years, real estate agents were relied on for their knowledge of various areas in which they plied their trade. You could consult with them as to the quality of the schools, where various ethnic groups were settling, and so forth. Obviously, if you were Chinese and spoke only Chinese, read only Chinese, and ate only Chinese, you would feel more at home in the Chinatown section. If you were Italian, just immigrating to this country, and had limited knowledge of our lingo, you would be more comfortable in the Little Italy section.

Now, this may seem like common sense. You just found a real estate agent, told him you would like to live with your countrymen, and he found you accommodations in the right neighborhood. You could read the menu in the area restaurants, the people in the local stores could understand you, and you could understand them. You could worship at a church similar to one in your country, the area bank or ethnic credit union would be familiar with your tongue, and you could have a brew or two in a pub similar to those back home.

Then along came the "do-gooders" and civil rights nuts,

and soon a succession of local and federal laws were enacted to produce Equal Housing rights. It seems that agents were accused of "steering" clients to certain ethnic areas. "Racial steering" then became legally taboo. I seriously doubt it was ever detrimental to any group and obviously, as I have stated, it was actually beneficial to most people.

If steering could really be done, all agents would have steered you to the highest priced listing they had *no matter where it was located!* With the new laws, you may not divulge any information regarding a neighborhood or the makeup of a neighborhood as to its residents' national origin, color, race, or religion. Now, instead of agents learning the character of each area in which he deals, he must learn this—*"I dunno."* This is the only legal answer he may give to questions regarding neighborhood makeup.

If the nice little couple moving here to retire in an ivy-covered cottage does not realize that the adjoining cottage is the headquarters of a gang of Middle East terrorists, you cannot tell them. Even when you know that if they buy this little dream house, the chances of their heads remaining attached to their bodies for a long period of time are remote, all you can say when asked about the makeup of the neighborhood is, "I dunno."

At times it does seem ridiculous to use the "I dunno" answer. I have been in many situations where the client asked me about the neighborhood amenities, and they were really obvious. But I chose to use the legal answer, even though the client probably thought I was an incompetent nitwit!

You can never trust a client. Many sympathizers of certain groups will act as a decoy, wear a wire to tape your candid remarks, and then report back to the group with enough evidence to yank your license and put you out of business. Treat all prospects as suspects! Nice country we live in. God Bless America!

The Cocktail Hour

You remember our morning technique of varying your route to the office? Well, now we are ready to reverse that on our way home. Get out the street map and mark five routes that each contain a local bar. You worked hard today so you deserve a drink, even if it is just a Coke. Neighborhood taverns are an excellent place to find potential listing clients. One thing to avoid at all costs, however, is creating the impression that you are a drunk. No one wants to deal with an alcoholic. Never have more than one or two drinks.

My technique with the taverns is to get to know the owners, same as in the coffee shops. In just one case, the tavern owner purchased a new luxury home from me, listed his present home, bought five small apartment houses, and eventually listed the tavern with me for a total sales volume in excess of $3 million in just over a year's time!

One of the best methods of becoming well known is to "buy the bar a round." This need not be an expensive gesture. When you enter, look down the bar. There probably will only be five or six people at a bar with twenty-five stools early in the evening. Most will be drinking local beer, so we are only talking about a few dollars. This is a very cheap way to give out some business cards and make several acquaintances. No one will remember that there were only a few people in the bar, but everyone will remember this Big Realtor coming in and saying "Buy the bar a round."

An excellent tavern to frequent is one that is near a major industry that is laying off or adding help. Many times you will run into someone who was just laid off and is moving to another area where his type of work is more readily available. I usually try to spend about an hour each night at a tavern on the way home. Any more time than that would be counterproductive. I have slipped a time or two, however.

Be sure the bars are active, but not the ones that cater to winos, derelicts, deviates, and pensioners. You don't want to get mugged or panhandled. I vary my stops to include all types: gay, straight, topless, neighborhood, and the elite. Remember, all types of people buy and sell houses. Don't avoid a certain segment, or you may lose that business.

When you are in a bar, don't stay in one place. Work the bar just as a hooker would. If you don't know how a hooker works the bar, watch one or hire one (for advice on her technique, that is).

A lot of people you meet in the bars will be bullshit artists trying to impress, and they may even get you to believe their story about owning an apartment project they are interested in selling. Be sure to check out all details with the local assessor before you spend a lot of time on a dead-end listing. After a few bouts with the bullshit artists, you will develop a sense of who is on the level. Working the bars is a good technique and even works better than working a church congregation (it's hard to buy a round or talk in a church), and it certainly is more fun.

Incidently, that hooker you observed or hired makes a lot of money. Tax-free money. *Big* money. She probably thinks she cannot buy a house. Wrong! You can sell her an assumable or owner finance with ease. Don't let her get away. I have sold many houses to hookers and it has been profitable. Remember, owning a home is the American Dream. God Bless America!

THE "PAD" CAPER

If you have ever sold or shown a house, you have seen "the pad." The buyer shows up with a yellow, lined pad. Sometimes it is on a clipboard, sometimes on a nice leather clipboard if the buyer is wearing a suit. As they look at the house, they write things down.

I don't really know what they write on the pad, but it has always been interesting to me. I have tried to look over their shoulder to see what they write, but I believe most buyers are former KGB agents, because as soon as I sneak up behind them and try to see what they wrote, they clutch the pad against their chest. I have also tried getting them in a position where I could look in a mirror over a mantel or medicine cabinet, but they always tip the pad so I can't read it. When I walk out to their car with them and they get in and lay the pad on the seat, they always lay it with the writing down. One client left it on the seat with the writing up, but before I could read it he closed my nose in the electric window.

I found out you can get the exact formula for making an atomic bomb in the public library, but I have spent twenty years without success trying to find out what a buyer writes on that pad. I have personally purchased several hundred houses and apartment buildings without ever using a pad, so I know it can be done, but in writing this book, I wanted to pass on to you every little bit of information I could. I felt compelled to mention the pad, even though I have been unsuccessful in seeing what is on it. Maybe you will be luckier than me. If you ever get a copy of the information on the pad, please send me a copy so I can die happy.

Expired Listings

If you are just starting out, expired listings are a good way to get started. Some of the reasons are:

1. You already know they want to sell the hacienda.

2. You already know the price at which it won't sell.

3. You already have all the dope on the dwelling on a print-out or listing form from the previous listing.

4. They probably are dissatisfied with the present lister because he did not sell their overpriced hovel.

How do you go about listing this prize? Do you call up and say, "Hey, your listing is expired. Do you want to list it with me? I just got my license!" I don't think so.

Try this approach: "Hello Mr. Homeowner, this is Super Salesman from Galaxy Realty. A client of mine selected your property from several I gave him last week, and I would like to make an appointment to show it today at about 4:30 P.M. Is that okay with you?" His answer will be, "Yeah, sure, that's fine." You say, "Okay, see ya at 4:30" and hang up. Wait about fifteen minutes and then call back. "Mr. Homeowner, this is Super Salesman. I just noticed this listing expired yesterday. Has it been relisted?" If the answer is "No,", you indicate that you would be "happy to come over at 4 P.M. and list it, so you will still be able to show it to the buyer at 4:30 P.M." You have got yourself a listing! Get there at 4 P.M., list it, and show your brother (aunt, uncle, wife, or another salesperson) through at 4:30 P.M.

What if he says, "Yes, I listed it last night." Do you confess to your motives? Nope. You wait until 3:30 P.M. and call back. "Mr. Homeowner, this is Super Salesman again. Sorry to bother you, but I have to cancel our 4:30 P.M. appointment. The buyer liked one of the other homes we showed him this afternoon and made an offer and it was accepted."

This saves face for you and instills confidence that you have buyers. Maybe when this overpriced hovel expires again, he will *call you.*

**OUR RECORDS INDICATE YOUR PROPERTY
IS NO LONGER ON THE MARKET!**

- WE WOULD BE HAPPY TO ASSIST YOU IN SELLING YOUR PROPERTY.
- WE CAN ARRANGE FINANCING.
- OUR MODERN, COMPUTERIZED OFFICE IS OPEN 7 DAYS A WEEK TO SERVE YOU.
- IF YOU WOULD LIKE TO LIST YOUR PROPERTY WITH US . . . CALL 482-3200 ANYTIME!

ANDY KANE REALTY
1942 E. MAIN ST. — ROCHESTER, N.Y. 14609

Another method that I have used is a postcard mailed to coincide with the expiration. The card has a "For Sale" sign with a question mark on it. It gets attention and possibly may be the first indication to the owner that his listing has expired.

Direct mail is far more expensive and the success rate is low compared to the "I have a buyer" phone call. But you can only call so many a day, and you can always have your wife addressing and licking stamps between changing babies and cleaning.

Getting The Actual Listing

All the groundwork in the previous portion of this book will be worthless if you do not obtain a legible, correctly priced, accurate listing contract signed by the seller. When a client calls you to list his home, never go unprepared. Obtain all the information on his property that is available from government agencies. Type all the information on the listing, including the dates, as I mentioned before. Since other brokers and salespeople will be using this information to present this home to their clients, your eyes are their eyes! If you don't put all the features of this home on this listing, there is absolutely no way that other brokers will be aware of the feature. The dog run or pool heater that you leave off the listing may very well be exactly what a buyer is looking for in his new home. If he passes over this house because of what you left off the listing, you may very well have lost a sale.

Don't "flower up" the listing with descriptions, such as beautiful patio, lovely fenced yard, spectacular, scrumptious, and all the other adjectives that take up valuable space on the listing form. Keep it brief but accurate. What you consider beautiful, lovely, etc., may be horrible to a buyer. An old associate of mine who was an artist would always say,

"Beauty is in the eyes of the beholder." Believe me, many things he considered beautiful I would gladly have thrown in the trash. So just keep it accurate.

Do not mention features just because the client keeps repeating how wonderful they are. "The water heater is new, the roof is new, the plumbing is new, etc." I have found over the years that "new" could be one week, six months, or ten years. Your credibility is in danger when the buyer reads "new" on the listing and then finds that the "new" item is actually two years old. He will place you in the category of the fast-talking, slick used-car salesman who tells you "it was only driven on Sundays by a little old lady." A professional keeps it brief and accurate.

Access to the property is probably only second to price in importance. Unless the house is vacant or the owner is severely ill, the owner's phone number should be on the listing so agents with potential clients may contact him directly. If the agent must contact you, and you must contact

the owner, you are wasting time that could better be used to get more listings. The shortest distance between two places is a straight line...right from the agent with the potential buyer to the owner. That way you are not bothered, or the property will still be shown if you are out of town.

You would be surprised how many times I have been out of town, having a nice time in Canada, Florida, or the islands, and returned to find one of my listings sold and a couple of thousand dollars or so due me as a lister! Obviously this would not have occurred if the agent with the potential buyer had to contact me before showing. Also, get a key, tag it, and be sure it is in the office so the property may be shown while the owner is away, too.

When you are listing the property, keep your eyes open for things that may or may not go with the house. Itemize those things on the listing so there is no question. Many deals die because the aboveground pool, the storage shed, the garage door opener, or the bar stools became a big factor later.

THE KICKBACK CAPER

An owner of a suburban trailer park (mobile home court to you classy guys) had his property listed. It consisted of a hundred or so sites (rented at about $50 a month *more* than sites at other neighboring trailor parks), a bar, and a small store. The books looked great, except we were a little suspicious of the high rents being paid for the sites. The best way to verify rents is right from the horse's mouth—ask the tenants. We did. They indeed verified they were paying the stated high rents.

The property was purchased and the new owner began collecting the rent on the first of the month. The first tenant came in and paid the rent. When he received his rent receipt, he said, "Where are my chips?" The new owner said, "Huh?" The tenant replied that the old owner always gave them $50 in chips when they paid the rent, which were good for booze in his bar or grub in his store!

It sure made the rent rolls look good for the new buyer. Beware; if something looks too good to be true, it probably is!

Home Sweet Home

Now you have completed a full day's work and have arrived home for dinner with the wife and kids, an evening in front of the TV with the newspaper, maybe a log on the fire, dog at your feet...wrong!

Everyone is home now. You can reach 90 percent of the entire population in most cities between 5 and 7 P.M. each weekday evening. Grab that phone and do some prospecting. Use the evening paper for some leads. Open to the unlikely headings like "garage sales," "household goods," "appliances," or "recreational vehicles." Call and ask if their garage, household, or appliance sale is due to a pending move. Many people liquidate these items when planning a move. Why recreational vehicles? Would you need a snowmobile if you were moving to Florida, or a boat and trailer in Alaska?

While we are on the subject of the telephone, was your wife there to answer the phone all day today? The answer is probably no. If you have spent all that time making contacts, passing out your cards, buying drinks, etc., and now the person you met this morning wants to list his house but he cannot reach you, you are in trouble! So get an answering machine. They are cheap, usually cost less than $100, and are tax deductible. You will get *all* your calls then. A good feature is the "remote," which allows you to call home and get your messages from other locations, like bars, bordellos, or sporting events.

A client who calls and does not receive an answer is very likely to call another broker. That's just human nature. People who live in a home for several years take weeks, months, or even years to make up their minds about selling. But when they decide to sell, they are always in a big hurry. They want you there in thirty minutes or less, just like the pizza man!

So be sure the client can reach you. Use a recorded message like this: "Andy Kane speaking. I am presently with a client, but if you leave your name, phone number, and the address of the property you are calling about, I will return your call shortly."

You have identified yourself. "With a client," which indicates you are a worker, and potential listers like workers. "Return your call shortly" indicates they will not have to wait long. Never, ever use a recorded message that indicates you are not at home. Many burglars call first to see if anyone is home. If your message indicates that no one is home, you are just extending an invitation to the burglars of the area, and most of them won't even buy a house from you!

If you have young brats in the house, instruct them how to answer the phone and take a message. If they are not capable of answering the phone, keep them away from it.

It is very rude to subject potential listers to kids who are not competent to answer a phone, and you will definitely lose this potential buyer or seller. Telephone prospecting from your home during evening hours is a very good technique, and it will pay off better than you think.

THE "LOTS OF LOTS" CAPER

Several years ago I purchased a parcel of lakefront land 150 feet wide by 390 feet long. A developer had tried to get a variance to construct four homes on the land, but it was turned down because of neighborhood opposition. The variance was required because there was a requirement that each new home be on a minimum size lot of 150′ × 100′. Incidently, most of the homeowners who were objecting to the development were themselves living on lots 40′ × 100′. They also had been using the lakefront parcel for swimming and picnicking for thirty years and wanted to continue their free ride.

At the time, my home was in this area, so it was convenient for me to build on this land, but the only feasible way to make a profit would be by selling four homes, not three. Obviously, if you divide four into 390 feet, you come up with ten feet short on the last lot. You had to have a minimum of 150′ × 100′ to get a building permit.

How did I do it? I sold the first lot 150′ × 100′ with an agreement to *buy back ten feet* at a later date. I then built on lots 3 and 4. Then, about two months later, I repurchased the ten feet from lot 1, adding that to lot 2. For years, the neighbors were out at all hours of the day and night with their tape measures and flashlights, measuring the lots and trying to find the "short" lot. They also checked the original deeds and found that all were for 100′ × 150′ lots!

They never found my ten-foot purchase, and I think if you were to go down to that area today, you would still find one or two of these neighbors measuring lots after they had a beer or two!

Setting Price

You have invested a lot of money, time, training, a suit, a car, business cards, and assorted gimmicks to get this listing. Don't let an overpriced listing destroy this effort. Owners generally have an idea of what property in the area is selling for. The information they base their figures on, however, is usually secondhand. Get the exact sale price and date of every home sold in the area in the last two years before you go for the listing. When the owner tells you "Mr. Jones' house across the street sold for $138,000 last month and mine is just like his," and your figures from the County Clerk indicate that the price was only $110,000, you can say, "Mr. Brown, we use only reliable facts and statistics to establish value, not hearsay. It is very common for a seller to tell his neighbors he received a few thousand more for the property than it was actually sold for. It is just human nature."

I am sure that when you sell your home and the neighbors ask, "How much did you get?", you may hike the price a bit yourself. If you have a crystal ball, get it out now. If you don't, then try the following.

Prepare a complete market value analysis of property in the area. Present this to the client and then play this game:

Ask the client to set the price for his home. He will not want to because he thinks you may have a higher price in mind. The dialogue should go like this:

"Mr. Jones, how much do you think your property is worth?"

"How much do you think it is worth, Smart Salesman?"

"Well, Mr. Jones, I am going to write the amount down on this yellow legal pad I have in my hand." (You lift up the top sheet and write something on the second sheet). "Now, obviously I can't change it, so tell me what you think the house is worth."

Mr. Jones says $132,000. You lift up the yellow paper and, lo and behold $131,000 is written down. Magic! You say, "Mr. Jones, I think you should be a real estate appraiser. You are just a thousand dollars over what I feel is a good asking price for your house."

Here is how it's done. You feel that this house should sell somewhere between $130,000 and $134,000. Before arriving at the client's house, you write on the second page $130,000, third page $131,000, fourth page $132,000, and fifth page $135,000, etc. When the client gives you his price, you simply turn back the page that is one thousand dollars less.

You say that this is not too scientific? You are right. Yet the client will feel at ease with the mutually agreed upon price. After all, two people thinking independently (you and the seller) have come up with a price based on a market value analysis that is only $1,000 apart. Give it a try.

THE BUYER IS IN JAIL CAPER

I had a buyer back out of a deal at the last minute. He was going to buy a mansion from me that had been converted to seven luxury apartments and one huge owner's apartment. The property was in a nice section of town and paid for itself. It would have been an ideal place for me to live, except I had just purchased a single family home. We had moved in the previous week and my wife was still hanging curtains and planting flowers.

I decided to buy the mansion. I did not tell my wife, however, because I did not want her to stop working on the house. I had to sell my single fast, and an acquaintance of mine, "Paula," a topless dancer, had expressed interest in owning a shack. I stopped by the tavern that her enormous chest was gracing at the time and told her I would sell her my home and hold the mortgage myself. I gave her the address and told her to drive by and take a look, but not to tell anyone I was selling this property.

I was back at my office about an hour later when my wife called, very upset, because a guy had parked his motorcycle out front and was walking around looking at the house! He was the kind you might expect to rob or kill you—beard, boots, leather jacket, chains, jeans, etc. I told my wife to ask him what he was doing. He said, "Nothing." I had him arrested five minutes later.

About an hour later, Paula called. It seems she told her biker old man about my offer to sell her the house and he just called her from jail! I never knew she had an old man but I quickly called the cops and explained the situation. He was released, they bought the house, and we are still friends fifteen years later.

For Sale By Owner

FSBOs are a difficult bunch to deal with. When they have a toothache, do they get out the old Black & Decker ¼-inch drill and start drilling away? Probably not, but I believe it would be easier to fill your own tooth than sell your own house.

Think about it. What is the first thing a buyer does when he sees the crude hand-lettered cardboard sign on the front lawn? He immediately *deducts* the commission from the asking price because he knows there will be no commissions involved. The seller is doing all the work—showing, negotiating, advertising, etc.—and he does not get *one penny* for his effort! If he had listed his joint with a broker, the broker would have done all the work the buyer was trying to do, only done it correctly, faster, and with better results.

Dealing face-to-face is a hard way to sell, and many buyers are lost because of animosity. The buyer offers less, the sellers have a fit, and the buyer leaves with his tail between his legs, never to be seen again.

I have presented many offers that were only 60 percent of the asking price and countered to eventually produce an acceptable price. The real estate person is the buffer, and that's what makes it happen. There are no personal feelings involved. You don't get insulted or mad because the offer is less than the asking price.

How do you approach an FSBO? First, let me tell you a little joke. I was returning from a PMA (Positive Mental Attitude) seminar with a sales manager and some salespeople. We passed through the neighborhood where one of the salespeople lived and on a corner lot there was a sign right in the middle of the yard, "For Sale By Owner." The sales manager looked at the salesperson and said, "Have you tried to list your neighbor's house?" He said, "He's not going to list it!" The manager said, "What about positive mental attitude?" The salesperson replied, "I've got a positive mental attitude. I'm *positive* he is not going to list!"

You approach an FSBO with a PMA and demonstrate to them that you can sell their home. One trick I have used on my first visit was to simply walk in, *not* introduce myself, and say, "I like this place, I'll buy it." Mr. & Mrs. FSBO will look at each other and do nothing. You say, "What do we do now!" This is the best example you can give them of how unprepared they are. They may say, "I think we go to our lawyers or something like that." You introduce yourself, sit them down, and tell them that if you were a buyer and they had agreed upon a price, you could now leave and, since you knew that you could get this home for $175,300, you would probably keep looking for one just as good for $172,300, because you did not sign anything or leave any deposit. Down the street you would find your $172,300 house and never come back.

Now if they had this house listed with *you* and the buyer expressed interest, you would draw up an ironclad purchase offer, get a large deposit, and have the buyer in the bank for a mortgage application today.

Many FSBOs overprice their place because they do not have access to comparable sales. Offer to do a market value analysis for them without obligation. Tell them they can use this to show prospective buyers. Once you do the analysis, they will realize you know your business and whether their shack is priced out of the market or not.

Mention that you *qualify* buyers. Tell them some of your formulas for qualifying. Notice I said *tell them*. Don't give it to them in writing or they may understand it.

Stop and pick up some brochures on mortgages—all types, all combinations—from as many banks as you can. Deliver this package to the FSBOs and tell them, "You will probably need this when you find a buyer." When they see the several thousand mortgages the buyer may use, they will probably list with you right then and there.

Some of the reasons (R) FSBOs give for not listing, and the comebacks (A) are:

(R) I have spent $150 on advertising.

(A) I will reimburse you after I sell your home.

(R) My sign was painted by Michangelo Sign Shop and cost $75.

(A) Same answer as ads, but keep in mind their affection for this sign. If they don't list, hire a JD (that's Juvenile Delinquent!) to steal it next Saturday night. Give this FSBO a call on Sunday and say, "I saw your sign is down. Are you taking the house off the market, or did you sell it?" Mention that you could let them take one of *your signs* until Michangelo does another one for them. If they take you up on the sign, tell them on Monday that you had nine calls on the sign, but of course you can't bring these people over because you don't have the listing.

(R) My nephew (uncle, cousin, brother) has a real estate license and sells part-time.

(A) Would you like to discuss money matters with the family? Do you want someone to sell your dump part-time, or do you want someone, such as me, who will devote *full-time* to your sale?

(R) I have several "interested" buyers.

(A) Good. We will exclude them in our listing. If they return and buy this house, you will not owe me one cent and I will even help you get a mortgage.

Don't give up on the FSBOs. Almost all of them eventually list with a broker, and it might as well be you. If you are in the area with a client, girlfriend, family, or hitchhiker, stop in front of the FSBO's house and point, gesture, etc., until they notice you. When they call you tonight, say that you just happened to be in the area with a buyer and you previewed their property because it is exactly what the buyer is looking for. You are the one they will call when they are ready.

Speaking of calling, have your drunken brother-in-law call the FSBO about 1 A.M. some night and ask how many bedrooms the house has, how much it is, and if he can see it next Wednesday around midnight after he gets out of his night job at the bowling alley. The sooner the FSBO gets tired of dealing with crazy buyers, lookers, and nitwits, the sooner he will list with you.

You may also mention that many burglars, rapists, and junkies visit "for sale by owner" properties to case them for valuables, good-looking women, or ready cash. This does not happen when *you* bring a client because you have identified them, have their phone number, and some history. The day after you tell them this, it helps if a couple of unsavory characters knock on their door about dusk and ask if they can "look at the house." (Hint: Unsavory characters are readily available at biker bars for a drink or two.)

Another way to list an FSBO is *not* to list it. You approach the owner and never mention their home—just find out why they want to sell. It probably is because they want a smaller, bigger, newer, or older home. If that is true, you assist them in that endeavor. You find their dream home and get an accepted offer on that property subject to sale of their abode. Once they realize that the only thing between them and living happily ever after is the sale of 32 Ugly Street, they will *beg* you to list their home! I have had this happen many times, and most even reduced the price when I listed so they could get a fast sale.

Cooperation

Many real estate agents play their cards close to their chest. They are afraid if someone knows what they have listed, they will sell it! Then they will only make $3,000 instead of $6,000 if they sell it themselves. Even when a property is multiple listed, they keep some of the information secret. They don't mention that the owner will hold a mortgage with $1,000 down, the present mortgage is freely assumable at a low interest rate, they have a key in their pocket and the house can be shown even though the seller is out of town for six weeks, and so forth.

My theory is that half a loaf is better than no loaf at all. I'll take that three grand and move on to the next sale. My seller will be free to buy and I will get a commission on that sale sooner.

I have seen real estate agents fighting over a sale many times, and it is pointless. The best offer will win out, no matter what.

Cooperation between brokers and associates is required of realtors by their code, and all agents should subscribe to this principle whether they are realtors or not. It works well and is one of the reasons that areas served by realtors and multiple

listing services are more prosperous for agents.

I have helped many associates make a deal on one of my listings. I have suggested ways to approach their buyer that would fit in with my seller's plans (closing date, terms, etc.) so the offer would have a 99 percent chance of being accepted. I have referred listings I felt I could not market to someone who I felt could do it, and the person I have referred these listings to eventually turned me on to deals I would not have found otherwise.

In a city with about four thousand agents and brokers, I can count the agents I do not have excellent working relationships with on one hand after twenty years in the business. Cooperation puts more bread on everyone's table.

THE WOOD-FRAME HOUSE CAPER

When I first started selling real estate, I had an investor who bought many properties for rental use. On various occasions I would suggest property to him that was of masonry or brick construction. Many of these were priced the same as wood-frame buildings and were better, in my opinion, because they did not require painting and would last longer. My buyer always politely refused to even look at the brick or masonry buildings.

One wood-frame building especially turned him on. It was the last house on a narrow, dead-end street. This street was off of another very narrow street. When fuel oil was delivered, the truck had to back down the first street, stop at the corner because it could not make the turn, and use an extra long hose to get to the house. My buyer carefully noted the access problems to this house and mentioned that if there ever was a fire, the closest the truck could get was a block away!

He purchased the property and, about a month later, the property was destroyed by fire. He was right. The trucks could not get to the property. By the time they got the hoses across backyards from another street, the foundation was all that was left.

His logic escaped me at the time, but I later realized a possible reason for his fondness of wood-frame buildings. During a short period of time, many of his properties were destroyed by mysterious fires, and the insurance company paid off more than his original cost. He was eventually arrested for arson.

Reduce To Ridiculous

"Reduce to ridiculous" is one of the best techniques for getting an offer accepted, getting a buyer to make an offer without hesitation, or obtaining a listing. It is the simple procedure of making a client aware that his request or requirements are ridiculous *without* offending the client. You must act as though you do not understand the client's reasoning and repeat it as though you are trying to understand it.

Here is one example: a twenty-two-year-old kid drives up in a brand-new, high-powered sports car and looks at his dream house. He likes it! You say, "Sign here." He says, "I better show this to my father first." You say, "Is your father a real estate appraiser? What's his name, maybe I know him!" If this does not get his attention, you add, "Did you show your father that speedy, turbo-charged roadster before you bought it? As soon as you drove it out of the dealer it was worth 20 percent less than you paid for it. If you didn't get his advice on something that is going to be worth less and less, why would you consult him when you buy property that is going to be worth more and more each year?"

By doing this, you have eliminated the boy's need to reinspect the property with Daddy and have saved yourself another trip to the property. The trick is to politely discredit the person that your client wishes to show the property to.

I happen to live in Rochester, New York, the home of Kodak, the film giant. Hundreds of thousands are employed by the great yellow father and, therefore, many young buyers' parents work there. When I go through the "Is your father a real estate appraiser" (or builder, architect, etc.) spiel and they tell me, "No, he works at Kodak," my usual comeback is "Ya mean he puts film in little yellow boxes and you are seeking his advice on a real estate deal?" Most people will forget about their request once you reduce it to ridiculous.

Here is some more ammunition. Let's say you list a property and the client does not want to give you a key. Not having a key will hinder your effort to sell this mansion. The client says you won't need a key because "We are always home." Your answer: "I have found after twenty years in this business that most families eat. Do you ever go to the grocery store?" or "I notice that you have three 'rug rats.' Do you ever take them to the doctor, school functions, grandma's?" or "I noticed you only have one jalopy. Don't you ever take your husband to work or the train?" I think we have now reduced to ridiculous their suggestion that they are "always home."

Prices on offers and counteroffers can be treated the same way. When an offer, counteroffer, or price is off by a few thousand dollars, reduce the amount to ridiculous. If a counteroffer is $5,000 more than the buyer's offer, mention that over the life of the mortgage the cost of owning their dream home is only (5000÷25 years÷365 days) fifty-four cents a day! Throw a pocketful of change on the table and tell them the first two weeks in their new home is on you!

Size and shape of the palace can always be reduced to ridiculous, too. If the buyer indicates they must have a guest room for mother-in-law visits, question them. "How many times has the old hag come to visit in the last year? Oh, it was three years ago! How old is she...eighty-two? Let's see, if she comes every three years and lives to be ninety-two, that's three more visits, and an extra bedroom in this track adds $15,000 to the basic price. That comes to $5,000 per visit." You can be sure that no one's mother-in-law is worth $5,000. They will buy your listing without the guest room.

Location is another factor you can reduce to ridiculous. Let's say they "have" to be near the park (lake, work, school, health club). Your reply: "Do you have a car?" Of course they do. Mention that it's noisy, crowded, and expensive to live near the park. "How many times did you go to the park last year? Twice? Hmmm, houses near the park are running about $30,000 more than my listing in Niceville. That breaks down to $15,000 a visit to the park. I go to Europe for $10,000!" Then explain that in most areas, freeways and thruways will put you within a few minutes drive of most desirable destinations.

Keep the "reduce to ridiculous" technique in mind and it might even work in non-real estate situations. Try it when you buy your next car, suit, TV, or anything else where negotiations are required.

"JOE. . . HE AIN'T DEAD" CAPER

I had a call from a lady who spoke broken English. She asked me to come over and list her home. I arrived and she showed me the place. As we entered an upper room, I noticed a hospital-type bed with an elderly man in it who appeared to be sleeping. The lady told me, "This is Joe." I said, "He looks dead." She said, "No, Joe ain't dead. He's just sleeping."

We filled out the listing contract and she signed it, then took it over to the bed and explained it to Joe, put the pen in his hand, took his wrist and signed his name. I showed this property several times and every time he looked the same to me. Sometimes his eyes were open, sometimes closed, but he never moved.

I finally obtained an offer and called the lady to make an appointment to present it. She screamed, "Come right away, quick!" I got there the same time as the paramedics. They were putting the electric paddles on the man's chest, an oxygen mask on his face, and hollering and yelling back and forth to each other. A regular madhouse!

Meanwhile, the old lady was quite calm. She looked the offer over and signed it. All this time the medics are putting the juice and air on the old man. They finally stopped and said, "He's dead." She said, "No, he ain't dead. He's just sleeping." She took the offer and explained it to him, put the pen in his hand and wiggled his wrist. The medics looked at each other, then looked at me and the old lady. One medic said I should add the time to the date, so I put 12:30 P.M. He said, "Good, I'll date the death certificate 12:40 P.M."

The old lady was smart. She didn't want to tie up the property or the cash in an estate settlement. It was the only offer I ever had signed by a dead person.

Investment Property

Many people will say *all* property is investment property and that indeed is true. But for our purpose, let's just consider income producing, multi-family, or commercial property.

Special attention must be given to listing this type of property because your buyer will not get sweaty palms or heart palpitations just driving by, as is the case with single-family, ivy-covered cottages. Buyers of investment property are looking at bucks, not proximity to grandma's house. When you list a multiple-family or commercial property, they are not interested in the color of the carpeting or the nice yard. They are interested in the income, expenses, and if this property shows any profit at the end of the year. Since your clients want facts and figures, your profit and loss statement had better include everything they need to make up their minds or they will not buy.

It's best to verify any figures the owner gives you for two reasons: 1. Buyers and sellers are liars, and 2. The buyer will always give you amounts *he paid last year.* Unless you believe in fairy godmothers and Santa Claus, common sense will tell you that this year's taxes, insurance, and related expenses will be *more* than last year's. The buyer is going to pay next year's tax, not last year's. Call the assessor and get the correct reading on taxes and charges. Your financial data sheet should include a photo if at all possible. A photo is worth a thousand words, especially when someone is considering laying out big bucks for your slum.

ANDY KANE REALTY — INVESTMENT PROPERTY

1942 EAST MAIN ST. — ROCHESTER, N.Y. 14609

(716) 482-3200 SALES • APPRAISALS • FINANCING

ADDRESS: 1724 EAST BLVE. — ROCHESTER
TYPE: ROW HOUSE
LOT SIZE: 89 x 270   ASSESSMENT: $375,000
ASKING PRICE: $425,000   CONSTRUCTION: MASONRY
DESCRIPTION: 4-3 BEDROOM UNITS. ALL HAVE NEW REAM GAS 100000 BTU FURNACES, UPGRADED
             UTILITIES. FULL BASEMENTS, MODERN KITCHENS & BATHS, OFF-STREET PARKING.

INCOME:

UNIT #			PRESENT	PROPOSED
A			$ 750	$ 800
B	(ALL HAVE		785	800
C	1 YEAR LEASES)		755	800
D			755	800
		MO.	$ 3045	$ 3200
		ANNUAL	36,540	$ 38,400

EXPENSES:

PROPERTY TAX	$ 14,900
INSURANCE	2,150
WATER	551
UTILITIES (PAID BY TENANTS)	-0-
MAINTENANCE & SNOW REMOVAL	1,155
MISCELLANEOUS	350
	$ 19,106

$17,434 PRESENTLY AVAILABLE FOR DEBT REDUCTION AND PROFIT. OWNER WILL HOLD MORTGAGE AT
10% FOR 15 YEARS WITH 25% DOWN.

THIS INFORMATION, THOUGH BELIEVED ACCURATE, IS NOT GUARANTEED

How To Find Investment Property Buyers

There is a current, up-to-date list of thousands of investment property buyers in your immediate area. How much would you pay for this list if it included the phone number of all these buyers? A grand? Five hundred bucks? A hundred? Would you believe it is available for thirty-five cents! That's right, and you can have this list delivered to your door each morning before you get out of bed!

It's in your morning paper! Open to the "apartment for rent" section and start calling the landlords who have an apartment on the market. If they already own one, they will buy more. Landlords will whine and bitch about the tenants. They will recount their latest eviction and how they are not making any money. But they will buy more investment property if the price and terms are right.

You should also acquire a Criss-Cross directory (a listing of phone numbers with address and name) and make a mailing list of investment property owners based upon the phone numbers in the classified ads. Eliminate those who are active in the real estate business. This list should be used about once a month to send out profit and loss statements on your latest offerings. It is also an excellent way to solicit listings of investment property, especially if you see an ad running for quite some time for the same unit. The owner may get discouraged and sell the property.

One of the things I personally like about selling investment property compared to selling little ivy-covered cottages to newlyweds is that there is no limit to the property I can sell an investor. If I sell him one today, I can call him tomorrow with another one. If I sell the newlyweds one today, I have to wait for them to reproduce enough screaming little clones to fill the shack before they will need another one. They are lost for five or six years. I can work with a nucleus of thirty or so investors and they keep buying and buying. Nice country we live in. God Bless America!

Welfare For Real Estate People

If you have not thought about it by now, you had better. What happens when you hit a dry spell? The last commission check is just about gone. Your plastic is charged to the limit. A little yellow slip came with your last electric bill, so you are stocking up on candles. You had to use a long rubber hose to siphon some gas out of your lawn mower and into your Cadillac this morning. You have three closings coming up but an abstract is lost. An attorney is sick, and an Indian is claiming that the land under the third house belongs to his tribe. So what do you do?

The trick is to set up your own little welfare plan in advance of the dry spell. You are selling real estate, so you find a nice two- or four-family and use your commission as the down-stroke. Although this property may not throw off a lot of cash in its early years, it will probably tide you over when the commission checks are light. I never could have been successful in selling if I did not have the backup income from my apartment house. The apartment dwellers also are a captive clientele for home sales—who would they rather deal with than their landlord? You coordinate the closing with their lease expiration. You can transfer the security deposit to the down payment. You are their savior.

If you decide to buy some investment property, let me recommend a couple of books that you cannot be without. *Care & Feeding of Tenants* is excellent from a landlord's point of view, and *Tenant's Revenge* will give you some insight into the devious minds of tenants. Both are available from Paladin Press and are two of the most informative, well-written books I have ever seen.

Another thing that you will like in dealing with investment property buyers and sellers is the lack of emotion. It's not, "Are the drapes staying? There is no walk-in closet in the guest room," and all that. It is simply a matter of money. Either price, terms, or whatever, it's always a money matter, not an emotional one. The buyer and seller are investors, i.e., businessmen. They are easier to deal with because they are usually more knowledgeable than the average home buyers and sellers.

There is also a larger chance of finding a "motivated" seller with investment property. Many owners are "absentee owners" residing away from the property, either in another state or nearby town. Since they are not readily available to maintain or supervise their holdings, many become deteriorated and a target for city inspectors. If you check records of building bureaus for violations and ferret out the owners, you may have a potential listing.

Servicing Investment Property Owners

I have found that most owners of small to medium apartment houses have other jobs and, therefore, little time to show prospective tenants vacant apartments. About fifteen years ago, I started a real estate company to only deal in renting these units for landlords. We show the apartment, screen the tenant as to credit, job, and past landlord history, and we draw up a one-year lease. A good way to call your expertise to the attention of landlords is a postcard. It's cheap, fast, and you can saturate the market using your mailing list developed from the classifieds.

Since you have a real estate license, you may even meet landlords who will buy or list through you. Many real estate people seem to believe that a real estate person is just around to sell single-family dwellings and nothing more. I have found that the rental business is a good way to put beans on the table. Obviously the commission or fee in obtaining a tenant for a one-year lease will not put as much dough in the bank as the sale of an estate on the seashore, but it may keep the wolf away from your door.

I believe nothing has helped my financial picture more in my career than my involvement in all aspects of rental property. Try it, you'll like it!

WE WILL SHOW & RENT
YOUR APARTMENT OR HOME

- We do all showings and provide you with a tenant, security deposit and a 1 year lease.

- We verify employment, check credit history.

- You save advertising costs and valuable time! No more 'no shows'.

- Low, tax deductible fee is just one months rent!

IF YOU HAVE A VACANCY...CALL US TODAY!
ALLSTATE RENTALS 482-7946
(IF NO ANSWER...381-9445)

(left margin) SAVE FOR FUTURE REFERENCE

(right margin) SAVE FOR FUTURE REFERENCE

Business Opportunities

Now that we have established that your real estate license is good for more than just selling two-bedroom Cape Cods to newlyweds, let's discuss another aspect of the business. When things are slow, grab the yellow pages and call some small business. Ask if they would be interested in selling if you could produce a buyer. Some businesses will be small "Mom and Pop" stores in rental locations. Some bars or taverns will be sold with the real estate for an added bonus. There are all types of businesses you can sell. I know many brokers who have made an excellent living dealing only in businesses. They operate on the theory that they like dealing with business people, the hours are usually better, and everyone has the desire to "get rich," so it makes the selling job easier.

Just like the investment property listing, you must be sure to garner all the financial data and check for accuracy. You will always have a hard time pinning down an owner as to his exact income, especially in a "cash" business where items are paid for in cash daily (no credit cards, checks, or charges). These entrepreneurs may not let Uncle Sam know of every penny they take in. It's not unusual to discover a shop owner declaring $10,000 net profit on his last tax return, yet his way of life indicates that he actually may have made slightly more.

Unfortunately, you can only indicate what he declares on his tax return as his profit last year, and obviously you cannot tell the customer that the owner put $300,000 cash in his pocket. Nonetheless, I have developed a way to call the buyer's attention to the possibility that the tax return is a little low. As I am showing the business to a potential buyer, I ask the owner certain questions:

"Fred, are you still living in the ten-room house with the pool on Snob Hill, or did you move to your new estate in Richville?"

"Sam, I see you have a new Rolls Royce. Did you trade the old one in?" (His answer: "No, my delivery boy is using it to deliver our pizzas.")

"Tony, is your son still attending Harvard?"

You get the idea now. Your questions are designed to call the seller's lifestyle to the buyer's attention without actually mentioning any skimming of cash.

Selling a business is also a little more complicated than selling a house. You have to analyze the business—is the owner retiring, or after he sells Antonio's 30 Minute Pizza to your buyer, will he open up across the street with Antonio's 29 Minute Pizza? You must include a "covenant not to compete" clause, such as "will not enter into a similar business within a five-mile radius for five years."

When pricing a business, there are several factors to consider:

1. *Lease.* Is it long or short term? Can it be easily negotiated? A buyer does not want to pay two million rubles for a "cognac" store that has only two years left on the lease.

2. *Goodwill/Blue Sky.* The name of the business and clientele may or may not be worth something. If it is famous, you may find it a selling point. If it is "Bob Brown's Hot Dogs," it may not be worth a dime.

3. *Fixtures.* Are they modern? Are they actually *owned* by the seller? Many companies will put their coolers, display signs, etc., in a business if you use and sell their products. Be sure your buyer knows exactly what is owned and what is not.

4. *Help/Employees.* The book may show a payroll of $100,000 that does not include the owner's wife and seven stinkin' kids. A new owner will have to add eight people to the payroll to keep the place afloat.

5. *Bribes/Fees.* In many large cities, certain funds have to be paid each week for "insurance" (otherwise known as the right to do business) in a certain ethnic area. If the owner's nose is crooked or his finger seems to have been broken a time or two, there may be some hidden expenses.

A good thing to do as soon as a serious offer is negotiated is to take inventory. If there are equipment, fixtures, coolers, machinery, and so on, be sure to get serial numbers. Many times a seller will switch his new automatic ice machine with a friend in a similar business, pocket a few bucks, and put the friend's thirty-year-old machine in the deal. Be suspicious during all dealings with business owners and you will be safe.

Some Additional Hints

If you are listing a business and the usual commission is 10 percent, and you are also listing the building that the business is in and that commission is 6 percent, you will need to determine separately how much the real estate is worth and how much the business is worth. Most owners will overestimate the value of their businesses; therefore your portion of the sale of the business will receive the higher 10 percent commission. Always *ask* the owner how much the business is worth.

You can easily satisfy your curiosity as to what the gross income actually is by checking certain items used in that business. For example, if it's a beauty or barber shop, they usually use one towel per customer—find out what their laundry delivers. If it's a bar, count the empty bottles out by the dumpster. A small store? A customer count will give you a per hour average, then estimate the dollar volume per customer.

Most vendors to businesses will tell you what they are delivering if you give them a buck or two. I have never found a liquor delivery man, beer truck driver, bakery man, milkman, or laundry man who would *not* tell me exactly what a business used each week if I gave them something for their trouble. Just put on your Sherlock Holmes hat and give it a try. Elementary, my dear Watson.

Farms

"Ah choo!" My hay fever bothers me just thinking about it. Cow chips, old guys in tattered overalls, old ladies in gingham dresses. I won't get mad if you skip this chapter and leave the farms for someone who has "4-H" after his name and three blue ribbons from the State Fair hog show hanging next to his real estate license.

I like people who make snap decisions. I have never taken more than thirty seconds to decide anything in my entire life and I like people who can do the same. Most farmers couldn't make a decision in thirty days!

It's not just that they are dim-witted. The farm teaches them to take a week or two to make just about any decision. When it's time to plant, they don't have to do it by 6 P.M. today. They can do it anytime within the next two weeks. They can think about it.

When it's time to harvest, they don't have to do it by 6 P.M. today. They can do it anytime within the next two weeks. They can think about it. When the tractor gets along in years, they don't have to buy one by 6 P.M. today. They can do it anytime in the next two years. They can think about it.

When you bring them a purchase offer they must sign

before 6 P.M., they cannot decide that fast. It's just not in them.

I cannot figure out farmers. I know tractor salesmen who tell me about farmers coming in for two or three years, just looking at implements (yoke rakes, discs, planting machines, etc.). They finally decide on one, pay cash, and before they take delivery, inspect it with great care. They insist that the two scratches be touched up before they will take it home. When they get it home, they hook it to the tractor, pull it up and down the rows for a week, and at the end of the last row, they pull the pin, drive away, and let it sit there rusting for a year! It costs $16,000 and they don't even spend $9.95 for a plastic tarp to cover it up! Look around the next time you are in the country. You will see machinery sitting at the edge of every farmer's field.

Today's farmer on a small family farm is just wasting his time. Big factory farms are the answer. Many modern farms are best suited for subdivisions and residential use.

If you want to fool around with farms and farmers, go ahead and kick a few horseballs around, but I really can't give you much advice since I avoid the farm segment like I would a diseased hooker. If you are wise, you will too!

THE EGG MAN CAPER

Several years ago I was telling a friend about a problem I was having trying to list some farms. He recounted a technique he used to sell vacuum cleaners. He would take off to another city with three or four cleaners in his trunk and five bucks in his pocket. He knew that if he did not sell the cleaners, he would not eat and would have to sleep in his car. It worked very well. He always sold the cleaners and never slept in his car.

I decided to apply this technique to listing a farm. At the time I was living in a small town on the Great Lakes, about seventy miles from the Canadian border. The main route west was populated with small fruit farms, an ideal test. I started out about 7 A.M. with my listing pad, some signs, and about five dollars cash. I made up my mind that I would drive west and stop at every single farm until I listed one.

After about eight or nine hours of talking to guys in bib overalls and corncob pipes, I was almost out of the country into Canada. All of a sudden I saw an old farmer up the road waving for me to pull into his place. I assumed one of the hayseeds I had talked to had called ahead and this gent was interested in my services.

As I pulled into his driveway, he headed for the house. I got out, went up on the porch, and knocked on the screen door. The place was dilapidated but definitely salable. He hollered for me to come in and I did.

He said, "Give me three dozen large!" I said, "What the hell are you talking about?" He said, "Aren't you the egg man?" Come to find out, the egg man had a jalopy just like mine. I said, "No, I'm a realtor looking to list a farm." He said, "Well, I'll list the place. I got 50 acres, a barn and shed on this side of the road, and 125 acres on the other side of the road." I signed him up, put up the signs, and headed home.

End of the story? Nope!

The next morning I got a call from the farmer's attorney. He said the old guy was nuts, but he thought it would be good if he could sell the place and get into an old folks home with the proceeds, so for me to go ahead and try to sell it. (When someone is looney tunes, you can't enter into a contract with them because it takes two sane people to make a contract valid.) The attorney told me to contact him if I got an offer. About a week later an oil company bought the land on the opposite side of the road for a convenience and gas store, so my efforts were not in vain. This experience was my one and only listing and sale of farmland in my entire real estate career.

Turn Ugly Ducklings Into Swans!

Unless you stub your toe on a gold brick that just fell through a hole in an armored truck, you will never be so lucky as when you are called to list a run-down house in an average or good neighborhood.

Many real estate people are repulsed when they enter a property that has been severely neglected by an elderly owner for lack of funds. They know this property is in a caviar neighborhood yet is going to sell for a tuna fish price, thus their commission is going to be a pittance of what a luxury home sale would bring.

I look upon the discovery of a hovel in a good neighborhood as a gift from God. I negotiate a price with the owner to sell it directly to me. This eliminates inspections by buyers, bank-required repairs, and delays in selling due to bad conditions, plus the buyer is free to relocate immediately. I usually make the contract subject to immediate possession so that I may start renovation immediately. This is money!

I allow the seller to leave the property in any condition they want. If they are pack rats and have thousands of bags of junk, they can leave it and we will discard it. All they have to do is take what they need and hit the road. This makes

it very easy for them because they do not have to clean up the place, as a regular sale would probably require. I explain that our renovation is going to require a huge dumpster, so it will be easy for my guys to throw their leftovers in the dumpster.

I do, however, look over the remains very carefully, especially when dealing with old people who are prone to hide money and valuables in old books, bags, bureaus, boxes, purses, and shoes. (My record so far in scavenging through crap has been $6,800 in cold cash!) You should do this yourself before any winos you have working for you get into it. Otherwise, they may be the ones to find the goodies and forget to tell you.

When presenting my offer to buy the property, I usually explain to the owner that the property is "unmortgageable," which it is in its present condition. I recommend that they accept a token down payment from me and hold the mortgage for one year, amortized for ten or fifteen years. This gives me time to renovate and sell or refinance, and the payments don't kill me. Since this is common sense and easy to understand, most sellers go along with it. They actually don't have many options other than taking the distress sale price.

I tastefully renovate the property, taking special care with the following:

1. *Attic and basement* are completely cleaned, washed, and disinfected. An attic should also have three or four boxes of moth balls tossed into spaces in the eaves so that the aroma will be present. A good smelling disinfectant is used on the basement floors and walls.

2. *Heating, plumbing, and electricity* are brought up to codes and modernized.

3. *Walls and ceilings* are scraped, patched, and painted off-white to allow for any type of furniture the buyer may have.

4. *Floors.* Put new ones in the kitchen and bath, unless they are already perfect. Refinish any hardwood and check carpets carefully. If carpets can be rejuvenated through cleaning, I leave them. If they need replacing, I carefully measure each room and go to a carpet supplier with the exact dimensions. I carefully purchace remnants or discontinued styles the carpert supplier has. My first words when I enter his store are, "Show me what you really want to get rid of." The remnants and roll ends should blend well together: brown, beige, brown with orange, etc. I then hire an installer so the cost is kept to a minimum.

5. *Sags, bows, major water problems, and foundation repairs* are all eliminated. Any doors that do not fit because the property has settled are trimmed and refitted. If the foundation needs repairs in one area, I clean and point the foundation all around the house so the repairs are not evident. Sagging beams or floors are jacked up and secured. Any water in the basement is taken care of by waterproofing.

6. *Exterior of the house* is made to look like new with paint, siding, or new combination windows.

7. *Yard, driveway, and garage* are placed in excellent condition by planting, painting, and landscaping. Any bare patches in the yard are reseeded and watered daily.

When I complete the renovation, I have a couple of people clean the property top to bottom. All windows are washed inside and out, and the property sparkles.

I have seen many people who rehab a property do too much. Before starting you should sit down and estimate the cost of the renovations you plan, add this to the acquisition cost, and decide if your finished product is going to cost more than the area will bear. If it is, you can tone down some of your ideas. Paint instead of siding, less cabinets in the kitchen, etc. You certainly don't want to invest more than the property is worth.

It is not a good idea to change the character of the original dwelling. If it's a 1930s colonial, renovate to the original style, with the possible addition of a modern kitchen and bath. Old oak or walnut trim adds character. Refinished hardwood floors are an excellent selling point. Wallpaper covers many imperfections and is classy. A ceiling fan will bring back memories of *Casablanca*. Many decorative fireplaces can be converted to working fireplaces by installing a chimney on the outside, knocking through the wall, and fire bricking the old fireplace. Removing kitchen doors, and widening to archways will make rooms appear larger. Light colors will also do this.

A 1950 ranch is an ideal candidate for skylights. They can be added to a kitchen and living room to allow light in and make rooms appear larger.

Since I have extensive knowledge of rehabing and home construction, I personally supervise all phases of any renovation I do. This saves me thousands of dollars since there is no general contractor to pay. I hire all the subs and labor. Much of the labor is in the form of friends, family, and tenants. They work for a reasonable rate and are happy to get the extra work and related bucks.

When you start renovating you will attract neighborhood onlookers. I never let them in the property until it is 100 percent complete. You can say it is against "insurance regulations" so as not to alienate them. Get their addresses and tell them you will let them know as soon as it's ready, so if they have any friends or relatives interested in buying it they will have first shot at it.

When I have a home completed, I saturate the neighborhood with postcards stating that the property is available and open for inspection the following Sunday. On that day I arrange several plants and vases of cut flowers throughout the property. Sometimes I just take some from my house and place them in the open house. Be sure the yard is manicured and the walks swept. I have had great success in selling my ugly ducklings turned swans, and many have sold for amounts even greater than my asking price.

The house shown in the photo had been occupied for fifty years by one family. The last paint job was twenty years ago. I had the exterior painted, a new roof and driveway installed, and landscaping added. The electricity, plumbing, and heating were upgraded. The kitchen sink—which was cast iron and hung on the wall—was replaced. The rest of the kitchen was gutted, and new cabinets and ceilings were installed.

The front and the entry are extremely important, so no expense should be spared in this area. Remember, the buyer's first impression is very important. I used only the best entrance hardware—brass numbers and coach lights, brass

knobs, brass mail slot, and wrought iron railings. I wanted
the buyer to decide to buy this house before he got to the
top step of the porch.

When this house was placed on the market, I received three
offers on the first day and *all* of them were for more than
the asking price! My profit on this particular home, considering the time I actually spent acquiring it and supervising
renovations, averaged $135 per hour!

Next time you run across a run-down listing, grab it and renovate it! You will be glad you did.

Direct Mail and Phone Computers

The one big drawback of direct mail is that it is not! Not what, you ask? *Not direct*—it's actually indirect mail. When you are on welfare or unemployment and you receive a brochure for a world cruise, a luxury automobile, or an offering from a local country club, obviously you have received misdirected mail. When you just purchased your home and you receive a letter asking you to list your home, you received indirect mail. Someone has spent a lot of money to reach the wrong people.

Many salesmen resort to direct mail as a substitute for door knocking because they are lazy. How many pieces of junk mail do you toss in the circular file? Probably hundreds per year. The response from direct mail is only 1 to 2 percent. That means 98 to 99 percent goes in the trash. Unless the mail is *targeted*, it is a waste of your time and money.

By targeted I mean mailing to landlords, investors, FSBOs, or homeowners whose listings have recently expired. This segment of the market will produce a greater response than a regular mailing because you are hitting those who may need your service or buy your listing. The response, however, will not be as good as a telephone call or personal visit.

If you go the direct mail route, be sure to tailor your mailing to your targeted audience. A sample of one of my mailings is shown here. This piece was designed to be sent to homeowners whose names appeared in the delinquent property tax list, which was published in the local paper. The envelope is printed especially to attract their attention with Urgent and Tax Notice on the front. I doubt that anyone who ever received this envelope threw it away unopened.

The letter is plain, simple, and to the point. Don't go into long tirades or you will lose the reader's attention. I use this letter whenever the delinquent list is published and it has

gotten great results. Be prepared, however, for the few irate homeowners who do not appreciate your solicitation. They may be downright abusive or even threatening. Keep in mind that overall, your efforts will be productive, so disregard the death threats.

Phone Computers

You probably have received a call or two from these machines. They are advertised as "lead generators" and the ad for their purchase will include a testimonial from a real estate person who says that he cannot keep up with all the people who want to list their houses so he is working twenty-five hours a day! I purchased a phone computer and used it with limited success. I made up my own script to be short and sweet. My script was as follows:

"Hello. The next thirty seconds may be worth $100 to you! (This keeps them from hanging up.) We are conducting a survey of the county (make them think it is "official") and we have only one question for you. Are you planning on relocating in the next five months? Please answer now, "yes" or "no." (Machine records answer.) If your answer was yes, we will do a market value analysis of your home's worth. Our usual charge is $100 but we will do yours without charge or obligation. Please leave your address and phone number at the tone. Thank you."

The script worked extremely well and the response was excellent. My computer also displayed each phone number dialed on the playback and this machine generated some good leads and listings. You will notice that nowhere did I say my name or the name of my company. This is to prevent "revenge" acts when you call someone's unlisted number and catch them in a moment when they would have preferred to be doing something other than grabbing the phone.

Many laws have been passed or are being passed to regulate these devices, so be sure to check before you set your machine in motion. I don't think you can sell many homes from jail.

Also, use the phone on a line that is not metered, as most business lines are. You can take it home and use your personal

line, as long as it runs on a monthly charge and not a per-call charge.

THE TELEPHONE REVENGE CAPER

I heard of a real estate person who was using a telephone computer with a phone number readout on the replay. Whenever he received an obscene reply to his solicitation, he simply made a notation of the number that gave him the obscene reply. After he accumulated enough obscene calls, he programmed these phone numbers into his computer and recorded an appropriate obscene retort. He then programmed his computer to begin dialing the offending number at 4 A.M. Nasty trick, but he said he slept well after he got his revenge.

Too Many Clients

There may come a day when you look around and see that all your productive hours are booked. Your appointment book is full of potential buyers and sellers from 7 A.M. to 11 P.M. each day. The techniques on the previous pages have paid off, as expected. You are the top sales agent at W.E. Cheatem & Howe Realty, and you feel you need help. Don't feel bad. About two thousand years ago there was a guy named Jesus. He had a similar problem in reaching his clients and he found a good solution. He hired twelve assistants.

Of course, employees were more conscientious in those days and eleven of them worked out well for him. Today, if you have twelve agents, six will probably quit after you train them! That's the breaks of the game.

Although JC had friends in higher places than I do, we had similar problems. My clients want to do business with me, just as his did. My clients do not want to be served by one of my apostles. They want the real thing, even when I explain that some of my apostles are better trained, have more experience, are nicer, better looking, and smarter! They still insist that I appear at their property. Whenever I finally relent and make an appointment, they inevitable ask, "What will

you be driving?'' or ''What color is your car?'' I answer, ''I'll be walking. You will recognize me by the large wooden cross I'll be dragging!''

You will have to wear two hats for quite a while until your apostles gain their own followings. You will have to run the office and sell, even though both are full-time jobs. Here are a few tricks to get your salespeople in the client's door:

1. Make the appointment as though you were going to be there. Then send your associate with this excuse: ''Andy wanted me to get on this right away because you are his personal friends. He had to meet a client at the airport who only has a short time to buy a home and is interested in a three-bedroom ranch just like this. He wanted to be sure your property got listed so we can show it to the out-of-town buyers.''

2. Be honest. Tell the client you are sending your associate because he or she can devote full-time, twenty-four hours a day to selling his shack. If you listed the property, you could only give it partial attention because you also have to run the office, take the secretary to lunch, take out the trash, and have a few drinks. Your agent, however, lives and breathes selling and has none of the other responsibilities of a normal person (even if they have a part-time job as a fireman, heating contractor, or exotic dancer).

3. Make the appointment and take an associate with you.

Tell the client that your associate is here so he or she will be familiar with the property. Then if someone is hot to see the house and you are drunk or in bed with your friend's wife, the associate can show it to the buyer.

4. Send someone who you think the seller will like to keep your appointment. If the seller just got a divorce and is a horny male, send a good-looking single female associate, or vice-versa. If the seller is into antiques and you have an antique nut on your staff, send him. A little investigation of your client during the initial phone call will pay off.

Owning your office can be a challenge, but it can be fun, too. If it ever stopped being fun for me, I would join a circus and get right out of the business. If you do decide to set up your own shop, the next few chapters will be of particular importance to you.

Your Own Office

Being in real estate, you have probably heard that the three things to look for in a house are: 1. location; 2. location; and 3. location! This is even more true when you decide to open an office. If you screw up on location of a real estate company, it will be even more serious than screwing up the location of a home. The home just won't appreciate in value and might be hard to resell. A real estate office in the wrong location will cause you to starve to death! That's a pretty severe penalty for making a mistake. You will probably also need the assistance of a bankruptcy attorney. This can be avoided by careful planning.

Have you ever called a strange area and asked a businessman for directions to his office at 507 Pinecrest Street, Suite 700? It probably went like this: "Where are you coming from? Okay. Take Route 490, get off at exit 12, take Maple to the fork at Spruce, go to the third light, turn on Walnut, six blocks to the gas station at Pine, go east on Pine to the YMCA, and Pinecrest will be on your right. When you get to 507, go through the lobby. Past the newsstand and the shoe-shine parlor, you will find an elevator. If it's broken, take the stairs to the seventh floor. My door has a crack in the glass, so you know it is Room 700." Obviously you will not seek out this businessman. Instead, you will let your fingers do the walking in the yellow pages until you find a similar business on a familiar street in that town.

When you look for a location, keep in mind the other old saying, "KISS," which translates to "Keep it simple, stupid!" What better location than *Main Street*! If the area you are going into has a Main Street, get on it. Even the village idiot knows where Main Street is. When someone asks directions to my office, I say "1942 East Main Street" period! That's usually enough, even for retarded tenants. If someone needs further assistance, giving the nearest cross street is always enough.

Of course, I realize that not all real estate companies can be on Main Street, USA, and many Main Streets have deteriorated along with the cities in which they are located. If the Main Street in your locale has gone to the dogs (or hookers, dope peddlers, and street gangs), please disregard my advice unless you are going to cater to some subculture. Also, if you are in an area where some major thoroughfare is more easily recognizable than Main Street (ie: Pennsylvania Avenue in Washington, D.C., or Hollywood Boulevard in Hollywood), you want to be on that drag.

The next best thing to being on the popular street is to be right off it. You can then subtitle your address for convenience—10 Monroe Street (Off 133 Main Street). Another good address is prestigious one. If all the nice homes are on Showplace Street, it's easy to find, and there's room to open your lemonade stand there, give it a try.

Keep in mind that whatever location you pick *should be permanent*. You are going to have a lot of expenses for signs, business cards, letterhead, stationery, pens, and other items...all with your address and phone number on them. If next month you decide the location sucks, you will have enough fuel for a very expensive bonfire!

After location, the next most important element is the type of building. Since your expertise is in real estate (I hope), you should *buy* your location. You will get the tax benefits, build equity, and be in control of the tenants in your immediate vicinity. You don't want a massage parlor or an adult bookstore as your neighbor if you are trying to attract some buyer for your listings in Niceville Center.

One other important item is income. The property on which my office is located pays for itself. The rent from the other units in the building pays all the expenses. Mortgage, taxes, insurance, and utilities are all paid by my lovely tenants. My office is absolutely *free*. If I don't sell a single house this month, I will still be here next month.

Now, if you talk to some other brokers in the business, you will find they have to sell two or three houses each month just to pay the overhead on the office. That's twenty-four sales or more a year just to have a roof over your desk. That's a lot of bucks down the landlord's rat hole.

Picking A Crew

Remember when you were a kid on the playground and you tossed a bat? Hand-over-hand the captains went until one got his thumb on top. He got first pick and took the guy with the glove, and so on until the little pip-squeak got picked. You had a team!

It's almost as easy to pick a crew for your real estate store. Instead of tossing a bat, you run an ad. You take nearly everyone that shows up, train them, let them spend some money on a license and board dues, try them out, and can the ones who don't pan out by the time the dues are due again. It's best to take some time at the onset, however, and eliminate those who do not appear to have the communication skills, personality, or honesty to represent your shop.

This is hard to do, and I honestly can't give you any ironclad guidelines. It's usually a gut feeling. I have never ruled out anyone because of their background if I had confidence in their ability. As I mentioned earlier, I have hired salespeople from all walks of life with great success. I have hired a high-class hooker who wanted to use her street name instead of the name on her birth certificate because that's how everyone knew her! (I checked and it was completely legal, since that was how she was known!)

I also hired our mailman, the guy who came to fix the furnace, a disc jockey, a bartender, a topless dancer, a few waitresses, a siding contractor, several engineers, an artist, a few retirees, some firemen, a few immigrants, some computer programmers, and assorted flakes. All performed with great success.

Another salesperson was fresh out of the Funny Farm. I was hesitant about hiring someone who had been confined in a mental hospital, so I contacted the local licensing office for real estate salespeople. The examiner I talked to asked me two questions. Does he have something saying he is sane now? Do any of your other salespeople have anything saying they are sane? I got the hint. Even I did not have any document saying I was of good mental health! I hired him and he was great.

Part-timers are also good for several reasons. They have enough money coming in to keep grub in the kids' bellies, and they have access to a captive audience—their fellow workers at the mill. There are 168 hours in each week. If they work a 40-hour job, that still leaves 128 hours that they can beat the bush for listings.

Classified ads are a good way to find salespeople. Another excellent way is to offer a bounty. Most real estate associations have rules and regulations that forbid brokers from soliciting other broker's salespeople, but do not forbid salespeople from soliciting other salespeople. I simply offer my salespeople a hundred bucks for each body they drag in. To keep them from dragging in dead bodies, my C-note is only payable when their prodigy sells his first shack.

If you want to run a first-class operation, you will need somone to man the fort while you and all of your salespeople are out showing, renting, and listing homes. If you are like most red-blooded males, your first thought may be to hire a centerfold to grace the office, and that may not be a bad idea. There are some problems with this approach, however. She may not be able to read, write, or type. If she is so fantastic looking, she may be pregnant soon and often. She may have boyfriends who tie up your phone lines. She may have kids that get sick and cause frequent absences.

Through the acquisition of another real estate company, I acquired two older women whose kids were able to take care of most of their own needs. I can't remember a time when the office was left unattended in the past fifteen years. They share the responsibility and work, alternating days so they both work about twenty hours a week. If one can't make it because of arthritis, gout, or a heart attack, she calls the other to fill in. If that fails, we have a weekend centerfold who can also fill in. Our weekend girl was hired based upon qualifications that were apparent (shorts, sweater, heels, etc.) as she walked by the office about nine years ago. She has now learned to read, write, and type, so she is very helpful.

I hesitate using "floor time" for salespeople for several reasons, one of which is that they are unable to immediately respond if a buyer wants to act immediately on a deal, since they are "on duty" until 9 P.M.

You should also keep your eye open for potential sales associates in your travels. When you encounter a store clerk, gas station attendant, or tradesman who seems to deal well with clients, give him your card and suggest he try real estate.

If he is in a low-volume, low-profit sales job (door-to-door sales, noncommissioned sales), suggest that the same time required to sell a brush to a customer in a door-to-door operation could probably result in a real-estate listing worth several thousand dollars in commissions.

A good office and sales staff is a necessary thing if you are going to make it in the real estate business. Good luck!

THE SLACK JAW, VW, AND PIPE CAPER

A few years ago I ran into a distributor of mobile homes. He had quite a large spread and represented several major manufacturers of huge mobile homes. He employed many salespeople, and we got into a discussion regarding hiring. He told me he never hired anyone who had a "slack jaw" (lower jaw down, mouth usually open, like a turtle catching flies), anyone who drove a Volkswagen Beetle, or anyone who smoked a pipe.

His theory was that "slack jaw" was a sign of stupidity. I have carefully observed anyone with this trait and I believe he was right. The VW Beetle people were not ambitious—they were too frugal and anti-American because they bought foreign crap. Again, I watched these people and he appeared to be right, although the VW Beetle is not as prominent today as it was a few years ago. And pipe...he asked me if I knew anyone who smoked a pipe. I did. He said "What do they do when you ask them a question?" I thought back and immediately remembered. They take a puff before they answer! His reasoning, and I concur, is they can't think fast. They buy a little time with their puff.

My friend not only refused to hire anyone from these three categories but he refused to allow his salespeople to talk with any who visited his dealership! He said his salespeople were instructed to ignore them until they left, or even turn off all the lights in the office and pretend to be closed! He was quite successful in the operation, so there must be some truth to the theory. I must admit that since I had this discussion, I have never hired anyone or sold any real estate to anyone with a slack jaw, pipe, or Beetle!

Advertising

When you open up your real estate office, the first people through your door are going to be salespeople, not buyers and sellers fighting for your services. A new shingle attracts salespeople like honey attracts bears. Many of these peddlers will be more astute at their profession than you. As a result, you will have to enlarge your office next week to accommodate the thousands of key chains, embossed pens, baseball hats and visors with your name across them, T-shirts, yardsticks, calendars, lighters, and coffee mugs that the slippery guys made you believe you could not do without. You should also contact a good bankruptcy attorney because when the bill comes next month for the advertising gimmicks, you will need him.

Let's break advertising down to three things: Agency (buy your home from Andy Kane Realty, located at . . .); Product (47 Nice Street, 3-bedroom, 2-bath, etc.); and Giveaway (key chains, rabbit's feet, T-shirt, etc.).

Agency
This type of advertising is good, but it should be considered secondary when starting out. The agency ad builds up your

company name, but it does not sell a particular property. It's nice, if it's cheap enough, but the results are hard to measure. If you are a sports nut and frequent a baseball park three times a week to smoke your cigar so your wife doesn't toss you out of the house, a baseball program would be a good place to advertise. This, in conjunction with your presence and a few well-placed drinks, will probably get you some results in the form of a listing or sale. I have successfully used ads in racing programs, circus programs, and other local events to make my company known in the area.

It is a good idea to ask callers where they heard of you or what ads they saw. This will give you some idea of the value of your advertising buck. If you are advertising in a program, jockey for position. If the front cover is available, grab it. If you can't, try for the back cover. Inside of either cover is next choice, and if only inside pages are available, you want the upper right.

Position of ad should be specified in any contract you sign. Then if they screw up, you won't have to pay a cent. It's also a good idea to have your ads ready for publication in advance. Have photostats made so your ad will be exactly like you want. Keep a file full of different styles that can be enlarged or reduced to fit the space purchased.

Product Ads

In this case, it's your latest listing. The daily classified is one of the best places to put your ad. Check circulation carefully before you decide what paper you are going to use.

28

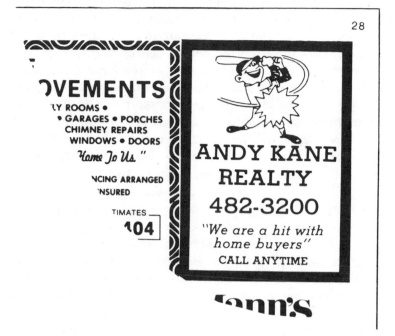

A dollar a line may seem like a hell of a deal in a paper that has a circulation of a hundred thousand, but it's no bargain if you can get in a paper with a million circulation for $1.98 a line! Always question the person selling you the ad as to the paper's circulation and readership (readership is usually much higher than circulation because circulation is one paper delivered to one address, while readership is determined by how many people at that same address read the same paper).

This technique will help you decide which fish wrapper gives you the best response. Either use a different phone number than your main number or advertise a property that is not advertised in any other media. Keep track of the number of calls you get on the test property and evaluate if it's worth running other ads the next Sunday.

Many real estate people believe an ad should be huge, but I have had luck with the smallest ads, as long as they gave enough information to create some interest in calling. Once they call, you can go over all the juicy details of this dream house.

Some papers are targeted for a certain segment of the population, and you may have to spend a little more time researching before you decide to use one of these specialized rags. Take, for instance, a paper devoted to senior citizens. Check the actual mailing of this paper. If 90 percent is delivered to a senior citizen home or complex, forget it. If a large number go to individual homes, it may be a good bet since old geezers can't keep their shacks forever. Check 'em out.

Giveaways

This is the category of T-shirts, pens, hats, etc. If done right, it can get you some good exposure. You don't want your name on something that sits in a drawer and gets used once a year, like a corkscrew or a fishing bobber. You want your name out where it gets looked at all day, every day. That gets you the most for your buck. Below are some things I have used with remarkable results:

1. *Calendars*. Huge ones for business locations are ideal.

They must be big enough to be read from thirty feet away so a motorist waiting in a long line at the Department of Motor Vehicles has to stare at your name until his eyes bug out. I have used small household calendars with limited success, but these have to have a place to write in daily reminders so Grandma's appointment to get defleaed does not get overlooked.

2. *T-shirts*. Excellent! I have gone through eight thousand T-shirts and they have caused quite a stir at times. I always order a large amount of girl's shirts. There is no better place to advertise than on the chest of a teenybopper with a set of 38-Ds! For my rental company, Allstate Rentals, I borrowed the Allstate Insurance Company motto, "You are in good hands with Allstate" and placed the motto on the front. I also rearranged the hands slightly to appear to be grabbing the wearer's boobs. These shirts went over like hotcakes, and I could not keep them in stock more than a day.

3. *Yardsticks*. Not bad either, but only seen by the homeowner when he measures for curtains. I liked them for another reason, though. When I canvassed a neighborhood, I would hold the yardstick like a cane with the bottom against the porch floor. When the homeowner opened the door, I handed him the yardstick with a quick flick of the wrist. Now he's inside the door holding one end, and I'm outside holding the other end. I don't let go. He has to listen to my pitch because he can't close the door with the yardstick in it! Try to use gimmick-advertising only to its best advantage and cost effectiveness.

THE TWO-BATH CAPER

I had an open house advertised for a Sunday afternoon. The response was great, and I had many lookers throughout the afternoon. Most had gone to three or four before this and continued on to five or six more. It was probably a very confusing day for homebuyers trying to remember the good features of all the houses they viewed.

Early Monday, a couple called me and said they would like to come in as soon as possible to write an offer on my listing.

A half hour later we were sitting down and writing up the offer. The wife mentioned that of all the homes they looked at, they decided on this one because it "had two baths." I tried not to drop my pen, because the house they were buying *only had one bath*! Obviously they were confusing this one with another one they had seen.

I try not to ever disagree with a client, so I did not mention the one bath to them. What happened when they took title and moved in? Absolutely nothing. I expected a call saying someone had stolen a bathroom, or the sellers took it with them, but when they moved in absolutely nothing happened. I think they were too embarrassed to say anything.

Traffic Builders

Office traffic is a must for every real estate office. This traffic will usually build up during certain periods, and you won't have to do anything except qualify the buyer and get his name on the dotted line to make moolah. What to do when things are slow and no one is coming in the front door? Put out some bait just like any good hunter!

Over the years I have used many techniques to entice flies into my web. On one occasion I had my voluptuous weekend secretary (42-26-34) wash the windows on the front of the office in a tight sweater and shorts. This attracted a few new visitors to the premises, and I was able to convert a curiosity seeker or two into renting or buying the residence of their dreams.

Holidays are a dreadful time in the real estate profession. Most live ones would rather prop up in front of the tube and watch a bunch of fat jackasses with numbers on their backs throw a ball around, rip a feathery bird apart at the dining room table, or open a package of gift-wrapped argyle socks. Anticipating the holiday hell, I used my free time to design and erect a 8' × 10' sign on top of a one-story building on Main Street. The sign was just beyond an overpass that raised street traffic over a railroad track. As you came over the overpass, your windshield was filled with my catchy sign. You would have to be blind to miss it.

This street was one of the most heavily traveled in the area, and I would estimate that 90 percent of the population saw my sign in the next thirty days. It was a good advertising ploy, but I wanted to get these prospects out of their Toyotas and into my office. I ran an ad in the local fish wrapper and offered a FREE GIFT if the reader could tell us where the sign was located!

The response was tremendous. The "free gift" was a pen with our logo and advertising on it (cost: nineteen cents). We obtained seven new listings and four sales, for a total revenue of $16,345. Notice that, though the sign had my phone number, the ad *did not*. It just had my address, so they had to *come in* the office to get their free gift.

The day the ad appeared it was snowing, blowing, and about ten degrees outside. Can you imagine hitching up the dog team and plowing through the white stuff to 1942 East Main and your reward is a nineteen-cent ball-point pen! Some people were abusive, and one excitable gentleman was extremely ungrateful after being awarded his prize. I said, "What did you expect, a new car?"

This got me thinking. Thousands of readers had seen the

Page 16 the Eastsider, Wed., Dec. 9, 1987

NEW CAR . . . .

On Nov. 21, We Ran The 'Have You Seen The Sign Contest'. B. A. Perrault Of Newbury St., Shown Here With Her New Car, Was The First One With The Correct Answer. If You Are Considering Selling Your Home, Call ANDY KANE REALTY 482-3200.

ad but not responded. They had no idea what cheap prize I awarded to those who responded. It *could* have been a new car for all they knew. One of my salespeople had just bought a new Cadillac...my mind never stops! If readers *thought* I gave away a Caddie, they certainly would respond to future gimmicks without hesitation. I gave my salesgal a call and told her to get her jalopy washed and get over to the office for a photo session. The following ad appeared two weeks later.

Notice the ad does not say *say* I gave away a new car. It just says she *has* a new car. I would never resort to a false ad, but I would bet that 99 percent of the readers would swear on a stack of Bibles that Andy Kane Realty gave away a new car just for being the first one to respond to the November 21st ad!

The whole advertising program, done in one of the slowest months of the year, generated over sixteen grand in profit with a total cost of just $246.50, including the cheap pens, the cost of the ad, and having the girl's Caddie washed!

Put on your thinking cap the next time you want to generate some office traffic. A hint: watch what car dealers do. They are experts. I have seen a guy frozen in a block of ice for forty-eight hours, suspended in a straitjacket upside down by a crane, sword swallowers, fire-eaters, jugglers, and ladies sawed in half in front of car dealers. See what you can come up with. (Maybe you could threaten one of your nonproductive salespeople with the saw!)

Signs That Sell

One of the first decisions that confront a broker when he decides to open his own real estate office is the FOR SALE sign! The FOR SALE sign is one of the most important tools that any realtor has to sell homes, yet many times the value of this tool is diminished by its appearance.

I am sure that if Michelangelo were alive today, many realtors would immediately commission him to do an elaborate work of art for their sign. How many times have you seen real estate signs that were cluttered up with a man jumping over a house carrying a sold sign, a tree, a map, a lighthouse, barn, keys, soldiers, or other distracting objects? These items do only one thing—they reduce the area that is available for the most important information...your company name and phone number! Even the words "For Sale" should take a back seat to your company's name and phone number.

Before entering the real estate field, I spent several years as an artist for a large corporation and had become familiar with the best lettering, designs, and colors to hold viewer's attention. I learned that *retention* is an important criteria. In a slide presentation, the slide is only on the screen for a few seconds. For a successful program, the audience must retain what they see in those few seconds. The same thing is true for real estate signs. A client driving through a neighborhood at thirty miles per hour must be able to retain the information on your sign with just a few seconds to view it.

If your name and phone number are in small print, weird colors, or buried among a lot of gobbledygook, you may very well lose that client. Very few will stop and back up, go around the block, or spend additional time trying to determine your identity from a poor sign.

Let's make a list of items required for a good sign in order of their importance:

1. Color. Very important—it must not clash or blend in with the terrain.

2. Your phone number.

3. Your company name and size of sign.

4. Choice of lettering.

5. FOR SALE.

Now let's break this list down and look at each element (as well as some others) in detail.

Color. Certain colors can cheer us, while others irritate or cause tension. Many times, client response is determined by color.

The great coach Knute Rockne understood the power of color. To keep his players stimulated during halftime, he painted his home-team locker rooms a brilliant red, the highest of the high energy colors! The visiting team's locker room was painted a restful light blue. Rockne attributed some of his success to the color of his locker rooms.

The color of the lettering, therefore, is very important. Blue, the coolest color, makes clients passive and tranquil. Red makes people spring into action. Do you want clients to be tranquil or passive, or do you want them to grab that phone and call you? Red or other high energy colors are the answer for lettering.

Background color is also important, since this makes up most of the sign area. Most books, magazines, billboards, and other signs designed to catch the eye of the public have white as a background. This is not by accident. Many studies have indicated that white is easier on the eyes and attracts the viewer. White, or another light color, is ideal for a background.

One thing to keep in mind: Don't use two high energy colors of equal intensity, such as bright red against royal blue. To check colors, place two samples side by side, and stare at the edge where they meet. If they are in harmony, the line will remain distinct. If they clash, the line will vibrate.

Avoid dark backgrounds at all cost. A dark sign is not visible in the evening, even if headlights shine on it. Let's face it; nearly half of every day is dark. You want your sign visible 100 percent of the time. Some sign companies offer reflectorized ("nite-glo") finishes for a small additional charge. This is well worth the price to increase visibility.

A background color and two other colors is ideal. More than that will confuse the viewer. Most sign companies offer prices based on two colors on a standard background, usually white or yellow. This allows the sign company to paint thousands of standard blanks in advance to keep costs at a minimum. The major sign companies will have a catalog listing their background colors and available sign colors.

Your phone number. Of all the action generated from a sign, 95 percent is phone calls. Very few clients will take the time to drive to your office just to get details on a property. They will call instead. Therefore your phone number should be large and clear. It should contain only the seven major digits. Area codes just clutter up the image area and usually are not required on residential signs. If you use a sign outside your area code, have one made specifically for that property.

As crazy as it seems, if you devoted the entire sign to just your phone number, it would be just as effective as anything else you could design. Even without the words "FOR SALE" or your name, people would get the idea from the lawn sign that the property was available. The color of the phone number should be something other than your company name to visually separate it.

I do not, however, suggest designing a sign with just your phone number for two reasons. People have a much more

difficult time remembering seven numbers than they do names. It may not be possible to jot down the phone number while driving, but names are easy to remember. They can look you up in the phone book when they get home.

The second reason is any good broker wants his name before the public as much as possible. So now you may get the idea of a sign with just your name on it. *Wrong!* Don't do it. If you happen to have enough signs around with just your name on it during the month of November, you may end up getting elected President of the United States as a write-in candidate. Being President does not pay as well as being a realtor, and it takes up a lot of your valuable time!

Company name and size of sign. One of the most common sizes in use today is the 18″×24″ sign. The large number produced each year by most sign companies keeps the price very low for both the cardboard and the push-in-the-ground, metal-frame types.

If your company name has only four or five letters, I would suggest a vertical layout (i.e., 18 inches wide × 24 inches high). If you name is longer than five letters, a horizontal layout is more legible.

A simple yard sign is ideal for most residential sales. A black metal push-in frame is easy to install by even your most frail salesperson. Larger, gaudy wood frames, which must be installed with a posthole digger, disturb the lawn and detract from the information on the sign. They usually necessitate installation by someone other than the listing sales associate,

and therefore create additional expense.

The 18″×24″ push-in or cardboard sign is easy to carry and easily fits in your salesman's car trunk. The sign can be installed immediately upon receipt of the signed listing. This exposes the property to the public several days sooner than if a maintenance man had to go to the property at a later date.

Choice of lettering. Old English, Script, Roman, and other fancy typefaces are excellent for use on your signet ring, luggage, or silver, but they sould *never* be used on a real estate sign. Sharp, crisp, clean lettering is a must. Some easy-on-the-eye typefaces in use today are Helvetica, Franklin, Gothic, and Futura. Visit your local art-supply house and obtain a lettering catalog for comparison of various typefaces.

Keep your eyes open as you drive our highways for typefaces that please you. Notice speed limit and other road signs that are erected by state governments. Much effort and research has already been expended discovering which typeface is most visible. I am sure you will not find Old

English lettering on a speed-limit sign.

The size of lettering is the next most important consideration. Your company name should be the largest. The phone number should be the same size as the company name or just a bit smaller. If you use FOR SALE or SALE, this should be about half as large as the company name.

FOR SALE. As I mentioned earlier, in most instances a potential client has only a few seconds to view your sign. Therefore, a minimum amount of information should be offered. Almost everyone who sees a sign on a front lawn will realize that the property is available. You may very well wish to leave FOR SALE off of the sign to give your company name and phone number greater exposure.

The layout. Using a piece of tracing paper or the back of an old sign, make a rough layout to scale for your new sign. Don't worry too much about your art work. Your expertise is as a realtor, not a sign painter. This layout is to give the sign company artist an idea of what you have in mind. He will create (usually without charge) an exact layout for your sign. When you have finished your rough layout, mark on it the type of lettering desired, size in inches, and colors, including background. It is best to include a small color sample for each color (except black or white). These samples may be cut from a magazine, hardware store paint chart, or any available source.

Mail or take the rough sketch to your sign vendor. When their artist has completed the final layout, they will submit it to you for approval. This is an excellent opportunity to test the effect of your sign.

The test. Take the layout to a local sign painter and have one or two made exactly as the layout indicates. Select a property in a high-traffic residential area for the test. The property should be one that will reflect only calls generated by your sign, and it should *not* be advertised, multiple listed, or have any other sales effort expended during the test period. If you do not have a property like this listed, consider your own home or that of a friend.

The test should last at least one week. Your phone should

be attended twenty-four hours a day, using a recorder or answering service for off hours. Make a record of every response. You should be able to accurately judge the response this style of sign will generate. If you are not satisfied with the response, vary type sizes and colors until you are satisfied.

Inserts. Metal frames usually have space for an insert. If your office phone is not attended after-hours, you may want to put the listing salesman's last name and phone number on an insert.

SOLD signs are a must. Put a SOLD insert in as soon as you have a sale. Although this will have the effect of eliminating any callers who could be referred to a similar listing, it will give potential listers in the area an idea of how long your company takes to market the property. If the deal falls through, you can always remove the SOLD insert.

Many sign companies offer a large assortment of stock inserts—2 bedrooms, air-conditioner, 1½ baths, fireplace— which can be used with push-in signs. We have found these inserts do not increase calls, but in fact *decreases* them. If a person must call to inquire if a certain feature is present in a listing, you may very well be able to refer them to any property with the desired feature.

Material. Lawn signs are usually made from 3/16-inch hardboard or 24-gauge metal. Our experience with metal signs has indicated that they dent easily, causing paint to chip and later rust. The hardboard has proven more satisfactory for everyday use, and usually costs about $1.25 less per sign.

Metal sign frames usually are baked black enamel, as sign manufacturers have found this color to last longer. Other colors are generally available.

How many? Most brokers begin operation with a limited budget and make the costly mistake of ordering too few signs. The silk-screen process is usually the method used to produce your sign, and most companies have a minimum order (six to ten signs). You should consider your needs for the next year and order approximately twice that amount. The price of push-in metal-frame lawn signs decreases rapidly as the quantity rises. For example, one company charges $26.30 per sign for a two-color hardboard sign with a black metal push-in frame if the order is for six signs. The same sign is only $13.10 in quantities of one hundred! This is an enormous savings and you *will* eventually use the signs.

Retrieving signs. Once the title has been transferred and a new owner moves in, the sign usually goes in the garage, backyard or trash. Educate your people to pick up these expensive push-in signs and return them to the office. A good policy is to issue the salesperson's commission check when the sign is retrieved.

Signs sell. Impress upon your salespeople that signs sell! Your sign should be kept neat and clean, just like your auto. A good-looking, legible sign is a credit to your company and will do much to build your reputation.

It is a proven fact that the person most likely to buy your new listing is someone who has reason to be in the area of the listing. A tenant in the area, someone who visits friends in the area, a son or daughter visiting parents—the list is endless. If you don't have a legible sign on that listing, you may lose that buyer.

Our policy is to place a sign on every listing. If a client does not want a sign on his property, I question whether or not he is really serious about selling. Our sign is placed on the property immediately upon listing and removed promptly when the title is transferred.

Classified advertising is expensive, it lasts only one day, and the neighbors of that new listing may not even read it. A sign will last for years and costs about the same as a two-day classified. Last year my office received 90 percent of our leads from signs! In a new office, this saving on classified advertising could mean the difference between success and failure.

When I encounter a seller who does not want a sign, I immediately drop my voice to a whisper. If we are in the kitchen and the window is open, I get up and close it. I look all around before I speak again. The sellers lean over and glance at each other with a quizzical look. I continue in a whisper, "Your secret is safe with me, Mr. Idiot Homeowner. I won't let anybody know your house is for sale!" They usually jump up and and say, "No, no! I want everybody to know it's for sale!" They usually consent to the sign.

Another good way to get your sign on a listing is to not mention it during your visit. After the listing is signed, just drive away. Have coffee nearby, then go back and stick the sign in the front yard without saying a word. Go back to the office, and when they call and say they did not want a sign because they "do not want the neighbors to know," tell them you will be over first thing in the morning to take it down.

Next morning, arrive to take the sign down. But say to the homeowners, "we had three calls on this listing from the sign last night. It's a shame to take this down while there is so much response. You mentioned your neighbors when you called. Unless all of your neighbors are stone blind, they have already seen this sign. Why don't we leave it up?" The answer will usually be "Yes!"

Vocabulary

This may possibly be the most important chapter in this book. There are many times when *one* word will make or break your deal. Some words should *never* be used in the presence of a seller and the same words *always* used when talking to a buyer. Commit the following examples to memory and your sales will show a definite increase. I'm not going to cover the obvious words (deed, purchase offer, etc.) because I know they are familiar to you already.

1. *Home*. A home is the cat on your lap, the fireplace burning, the wife running out to the refrigerator to fetch a beer, the kids' heights marked on the kitchen door. A home is something sentimental. A home is like one of the family.

Never, *never* mention the word *home* to a seller. If you do, you will just reinforce his desire to get top dollar for the sentimental value. You must do everything in your power to keep the seller's mind off "home." He's selling a *house*. Say "house" at all times when referring to his home. "I have an excellent purchase offer on your *house*" or "Mr. Homeowner, I will be showing your *house* today at 3 P.M." A house is a pile of sticks, mortar, stone, and carpet. There is no sentimental value attached to a pile of sticks, mortar, stone and carpet.

2. *House. Never* say "house" to a buyer. Your goal is to get him thinking "home." He's not buying a *house,* he's buying a *home*—a cat on his lap, fireplace burning, wife running to the refrigerator to fetch a beer. He will gladly pay more for a home than a house. So always use the word *home* in place of *house* when talking to the buyer. "Let's get an offer in on this lovely *home*" or "Mr. Buyer, I have an appointment to show you a lovely *home* at 3 P.M. today."

3. *Counteroffer.* Another word that can cause resentment is counteroffer. It causes the buyer to resent the seller. He didn't accept his offer and has returned a counterattack, counterpunch, etc. I avoid this word by using the following technique.

The buyer has offered to buy 75 Park Place for $175,000. The seven-year-old stove, the drapes, and the pregnant alley cat are to be included in the sale. The seller agreed to include these valuable items and sell for the fantastically low price of $177,000. I return to the sellers, who are waiting on the edge of their chairs, and say, "Congratulations! The seller accepts your offer. . ." I pause while they start packing and moving in their minds and then say, ". . .except he really must get another $2,000 to be able to relocate."

Your buyer will accept when you mention that $2,000 over twenty-five years is only twenty-one cents a day! The trick is to never mention "counteroffer." Always start out with, "He accepted your offer, except. . ."

4. *Commission.* Another dirty word. Both buyer and seller always resent the fact that for the three-and-a-half hours you spent arranging this deal, you are going to receive $5,685 bucks! If when figuring the seller's net you break everything down—your commission, his attorney, abstract update, mortgage tax, bank points—and discuss each item, your commission will obviously stand out since it is the largest item. I always lump all the seller's expenses into one category and subtract that from the purchase price to obtain his net. "Mr. Seller, after the *expense of sale* is deducted, your net proceeds will be approximately $171,355."

5. *Prospects.* When talking to a seller who is considering

listing his house, never say, "I have a *prospect* looking for a shack just like yours." The line is, "I have several *buyers* looking." Prospects are pie in the sky. *Buyers* is a more positive term and reinforces the seller's confidence.

6. *Gone fishin'.* . .Or on vacation, or to visit your mother-in-law, etc. Never tell a client, buyer or seller, that you are going out to enjoy yourself. This eight-to-five machine jockey will resent your going to play golf Thursday instead of showing him three houses that he cannot afford anyway. Instead, tell him, or have your office tell him, "Mr. Super Salesman has an out-of-town buyer coming Thursday. He must spend the entire day showing homes to him, since he must buy a home and catch a return flight at 7 P.M." This will impress any buyer or seller with the fact that you are active. If you are going to judge a beauty contest in Northern Canada and will be away several days, try, "Mr. Super Salesman is attending a seminar on creative financing (get it. . .financing=figures!) in Toronto and will be back on Thursday."

7. *Little; small.* Never say "little," "small," or "tiny," unless you are referring to a mortgage payment, estimating a utility bill, or taxes. Obviously if a bedroom is small, the buyer will see this unless he's blind. Don't say, "This is a nice little bedroom." Say, "This bedroom is certainly convenient to the master bedroom," or "Isn't this carpet lovely?" or "My, this window certainly gets the morning sun."

8. *You're wrong.* The buyer and seller are always right, even if they are wrong! When the client tells you something that you know is wrong, you will alienate him if you say, "You're wrong." You can simply say nothing, or as I do many times, say "That's right, but I think the proximity to the expressway will actually enhance the value of the home, since commuting time to the Big Apple will be reduced."

9. *Dampness.* No matter how much your feet splash around as you walk in the basement, act normal. Don't mention water or dampness. Act as though every house has some water in the basement. Many clients will think nothing of it. If the words water or damp come up, mention that a certain amount of humidity is good in a house. Dryness is bad for furniture

and sinus conditions.

10. *Neighborhood nuisances.* A firehouse, bar, school, race-track, or stadium may be just a block away. If you mention this, it may cause a problem. Many clients will buy a house across from a football field or stock car track on a Wednesday. It's nice and quiet. They will never imagine the noise until the first Saturday after they move in. Unless they ask, don't say one word. If you know what time a neighborhood nuisance is in full swing, just don't show the property during that time.

11. *Chemical hazards.* If you have knowledge of a past or potential health hazard, such as the "Love Canal" area of Niagara Falls, New York, you should acquaint yourself with all the facts so that if a client mentions "two-headed babies," you can put his fears to rest with "two heads are better than one" or "there were only three two-headed babies born in ten years." You will develop a certain respect for some words and phrases as time goes on. Just keep them in mind and use what works best.

12. *New.* Nothing is new. As soon as you buy something, it's old—one day old, one week old, one year old. It's all old, not new. Don't get into the trap of saying new. There are many other things you can say to create the same impression. Try saying "purchased last year," or "purchased new in 1989."

13. *Never.* Never say never! Never is a long time. If you say that someone will never have problems with the furnace, well, or whatever, you may find yourself in court paying for a heating unit or well that you indicated the purchaser "will never have a problem with it."

Conclusion

At this time, there are nearly one million people fooling around with real estate sales. You are on the right track to make big bucks. You have spent the time and money to purchase and read this book, and I hope you read many more because the advantage you have over the other one million people is knowledge. The more knowledge, skills, and techniques you develop, the more you will put in your pocket each year.

Some of the techniques mentioned in this book may not be for you, but at least now you are aware of them and will have them in your repertoire if the need arises. Real estate is fun. In most industries, you are put out to pasture when you reach a certain age. In the real estate business, you are actually worth more as your experience builds up, and I have seen many real estate people who were active in their nineties! You can ply your trade in any location at any age. Real estate is a truly remarkable and profitable career—go to it.

About The Author

Realtor Andy Kane has spent the better part of his life in real estate. His various companies own, manage, rehabilitate, rent, sell, or buy all types of property. Kane's knowledge and unusual techniques are now available to other real estate practitioners. Even if you have been in the business for years, Kane's tips are likely to increase your listings, leads, and income!